COUNSEL¹⁻

Concise, accessib'
counselling approa

This best-selling series offe﹏ ﹏ﬁensive descriptions of key counselling approaches a﹏ ﹏ contexts in the 21ˢᵗ century. Accessible and concise, they are ideal for students seeking a theory bridge between introductory, intermediate and diploma courses or for comparative essays and integrative theory assignments. Individually, they are perfect supplements to the *Steps in Counselling* series for students as they progress through their training.

The School-Based Counselling Primer is the first in the series to explore a specific counselling context. As such it offers the perfect introduction for students and practitioners and for school and education staff for whom this is a new arena.

The other primers in the series are:

The Person-Centred Counselling Primer – Pete Sanders

The Integrative Counselling Primer – Richard Worsley

The Experiential Counselling Primer – Mick Baker

The Contact Work Primer: introduction to pre-therapy – edited by Pete Sanders

The Focusing-Oriented Counselling Primer – Campbell Purton

The Psychodynamic Counselling Primer – Mavis Klein

The Cognitive Behavioural Counselling Primer – Rhena Branch and Windy Dryden

The Existential Counselling Primer – Mick Cooper

The School-Based Counselling Primer

Katie McArthur

PCCS Books
Monmouth

Published 2016

PCCS Books Ltd
Wyastone Business Park
Wyastone Leys
Monmouth
NP25 3SR
UK
Tel +44 (0)1600 891 509
www.pccs-books.co.uk

The School-Based Counselling Primer

A CIP catalogue record for this book is available from the
British Library

ISBN 978 1 906254 78 0

Cover designed in the UK by Raven Books
Cover photo © John Birdsall Social Issues
Typeset in the UK by Raven Books
Printed in the UK by Ashford Colour Press, Gosport, Hampshire

CONTENTS

Acknowledgements

I'd like to thank the young people, teachers, counsellors and researchers who have worked with me over the years, contributing to the work that has inspired this primer. With special thanks to Pete Sanders and all at PCCS Books, Mick Cooper, Lucia Berdondini, Michelle Aghion, Renee Clark, Karen Cromarty, Nancy Rowland and Duncan Kennedy.

FOREWORD

MICK COOPER

I think I was about four years old when I started to have panic attacks. Stuck on the underground between Notting Hill and Holland Park on the way to nursery, it felt like the tunnel walls were closing it. I felt sick, like the bottom of my stomach was falling away. Nothing to cling on to. No one to support or save me. Falling into a vortex that I couldn't escape. As I grew older, the fears started to emerge at night: lying awake in my bed, desperately attentive to every creak outside my room. Monsters coming up my stairs. Ferocious, vicious demons, coming to rip me apart. And then, around age 15, the monsters turned to health anxieties. Bone cancer, lung cancer… Spitting into the bathroom sink, convinced that I was coughing up blood. I remember getting really stoned when I was about 18 and having the worse panic attack of my life. It went on all night – my mum sitting anxiously by my bedside – and in it I had the image of a great big black iron gate opening in my mind, and all the demons and monsters that had been held behind it being unleashed. But that's what my mind was like all the time: a constant battle to keep that gate closed and the monsters, if only temporarily, at bay.

I talked about my anxieties with my GP. He was a lovely, warm man, with an interest in transgenerational trauma. He linked my fears to my mum's experiences as a young Jewish child in Nazi Germany. After a while, he referred me to the Tavistock Institute. I thought I was going to get help. Instead, what I remember most were the dents on the consulting room ceiling, and wondering if someone had managed to throw a ball up there. The analyst had one of those Yalom-like goatees… and just didn't seem to say much. And what he did say didn't seem to make much sense. He said, for instance, that maybe I thought he was like my father, and then he gave me a hard time for going on holiday and missing the last session. And

I just thought, 'Why would I want to spend the last session here with you when I could be with my friends?' It all seemed Kafkaesque, pointless, a farce. If this sitting in silence and glaring at each other was supposed to achieve something, I really didn't understand what it was.

Given the endurance of my fears throughout my life, it would be naïve of me to write that having a school-based counsellor would have magicked them all away. But having a warm, kind, caring person to talk to at school would have made so much difference. Why? Someone not to feel so all alone with. Someone who could have helped me start making sense of things. Someone who would have been with me in the nightmare lows – as well as the highs – and who I could come back to if things were getting really difficult. A place of sanctuary in a world that sometimes seemed to spin terrifyingly out of control.

And I would like to think that, if I was a child today (Spring 2016), things would be a bit different. For the first time, the government seems to be taking child mental health seriously. In 2014, we had the All-Party Parliamentary Health Select Committee report *Children's and Adolescents' Mental Health and CAMHS*, which led to the joint NHS England and Department of Health task force report *Future in Mind*. This established policy and commitments for addressing child mental health. In recent years, we've also seen the establishment of CYP IAPT (the Children and Young People's Improving Access to Psychological Therapies programme), the creation of the MindEd e-learning site, and over a billion pounds allocated to the development of interventions for child and adolescent mental health. As part of that, we've also seen a growing interest in – and commitment to – counselling in schools. We now have a counsellor in every secondary school in Wales and Northern Ireland, and new Department for Education guidelines on school-based counselling that state a 'strong expectation' that, over time, 'all schools should make counselling services available to their pupils'.

Katie McArthur's *School-Based Counselling Primer* is a valuable addition to these developments. It is a succinct, practical and accessible guide to school-based counselling in the UK. Perhaps its greatest strength is that it is grounded in the latest research evidence on school-based counselling: who it helps, how it can help, and the immediate and wider benefits it can bring to young people and their families. This is not surprising; Katie has been one of the key researchers developing this evidence base. Indeed, her research has played a crucial role in the development of policy and practice in school-based counselling in the UK.

More importantly, perhaps, Katie writes from first-hand experience of working with young people, and if I were a child, I know I would have loved to talk to her. Having worked alongside Katie for several years, I know what an empathic, attentive and caring listener she can be. These qualities really come through in her writing: her ability to enter into the world of the child and understand, and value, the totality of their experiencing.

Through works such as this primer, we are, I hope, moving towards a world in which children and young people can feel less ashamed and hidden in their mental health struggles. The monsters may never be entirely vanquished, but at least children and young people do not need to face them alone.

Mick Cooper
Professor of Counselling Psychology
University of Roehampton
April 2016

SERIES INTRODUCTION

PETE SANDERS

Counselling in schools is important to a range of people, including the young people themselves, parents and carers, teachers, and friends and relatives. This book is aimed at two types of reader:

- people wanting to learn about counselling in schools, with no previous experience or knowledge of counselling or psychology (some parents, teachers, carers and relatives)
- professional helpers with an existing general knowledge of counselling, who want a succinct summary of and straightforward introduction to counselling in schools (eg. teachers, counsellors, psychotherapists, social workers, psychologists)
- trainees and students wanting a brief introduction as part of their training or to help them decide their future career path.

Before we launch into looking at counselling in schools it might be helpful for some readers if we take a look at some definitions of counselling itself.

WHAT IS COUNSELLING FOR?

One way of defining counselling is to look at what it is useful for. In the past 40 years, counselling has become ubiquitous, and close to being presented in the media as a panacea for just about everything. Some critics say that the emerging 'profession' of counselling has much to gain from claiming, on behalf of counsellors and therapists, that counselling *is* good for everything. It would be wrong, or course, to make such claims: counselling has its limits and part of being a counsellor is to know what those limits are.

The problem is that, when we are in distress, it is comforting to think that there is a simple answer around the corner. The situation is not made any easier when we understand that simply sitting down and taking time out from a busy life can make things seem better. Counsellors must be able to explain to their clients, including children and young people, the differences between this very important relief and comfort that can be gained from compassionate human contact on the one hand and counselling as a specialist kind of help on the other. And readers will quickly realise that these two types of help overlap in many situations, including schools. Teachers already know this and may give a young person some quiet time to talk (without drawing attention to it) if they think the pupil is upset.

Counselling can help young people in certain states of distress and usually involves change:

- in the way the young person sees things or themselves
- in the way the young person thinks about things or themselves
- in the way the young person feels about things or themselves
- in the way the young person behaves.

Although many people, whatever their age, will not be able to put it neatly into a few words, what they seek from counselling can be roughly summarised in a few categories:

- support
- recovery
- problem-solving
- gaining insight or self-awareness
- developing new strategies for living.

The sort of distress that counselling can help is often called 'emotional' or 'psychological' and can include:

- stress – a very general and possibly over-used term, but there are some situations in life, especially those that you can't control, that might leave you feeling so stressed that it interferes with your everyday life
- conflict/bullying/abuse at home or school
- bereavement – whether that is the death of a relative or friend. Indeed, having anything permanently taken away might lead to a feeling of bereavement, such as losing your job or losing your ability to do something like walk, play sport, or go out with friends
- depression is another over-used term and not one to be taken lightly. Many life events can make us feel low, and talking it over really does help. The popular term 'depression' can cover everything from feeling understandably low after having your money stolen or not getting the right academic grades, through to being unable to get up in the morning or eat properly because you think life is not worth living
- coping with poor health, from missing school for more than a couple of days to having a long-standing or serious health problem
- trauma – eg. surviving (including witnessing) something very disturbing (including abuse of various forms).

WHAT COUNSELLING IS NOT FOR

When someone decides to attend counselling sessions at school they are, by definition, distressed. It is, therefore, particularly important that the young person doesn't have either their time wasted or their distress increased by attending something that we might reasonably predict would be of no help.

As we have already seen, it is difficult to honestly predict whether counselling will definitely help in a particular circumstance. Nevertheless there are times when counselling is clearly *not* the first or only appropriate INTERVENTION. It is doubly difficult to appear to turn someone away when they arrive because sometimes:

- part of their distress might be that they have difficulty feeling understood and valued
- they may lack self-confidence and a rejection would damage it even more
- they have been to other types of help and they think that counselling is their last hope
- they are so desperate they might consider suicide.

However difficult it might be, counsellors have to be completely honest with everyone, including the young person themselves, if they think counselling is not going to help. It would be wrong to let the client find out after a number of sessions: they may feel that they are to blame for not trying hard enough; they may feel weighed down even more by crushing disappointment, or they may worry that it means they must be 'really ill'.

The use of counselling should be questioned if it is likely that the young person's symptoms of distress are caused by:

- poor housing or homelessness
- poverty
- lack of opportunity due to discrimination or oppression.

Problems of this nature are best addressed by social action and working in teams. The counsellor should not be working alone, out on a limb, and should have, for example, medical and social work contacts whose help they can enlist with the client's permission.

It would be convenient if we could divide problems up into two neat categories: those of psychological origin (and amenable to counselling) and those of non-psychological origin (and therefore not amenable to counselling). However, there are some other causes of distress that, although they will not be *solved* by counselling, will undoubtedly be helped by counselling in that the person concerned will be able to function better with the kind of support that counselling can provide. It may also be that the client experiences repetitive patterns of self-defeating thoughts and behaviour that make them less able to deal with problems that do not have a psychological origin. It may also be that a person would be better able to challenge an oppressive system if they felt personally empowered, and counselling can sometimes achieve this. Such problems include those caused directly by:

- poor health (a physical illness or ORGANIC CONDITION)
- oppression and discrimination, including bullying
- living in an abusive family.

Counsellors must be constantly vigilant to ensure that their work with a particular client or clients in general is not contributing to disadvantage, abuse and oppression by rendering people more accepting of poor conditions, whether at work or at home.

WHERE DOES SCHOOL-BASED COUNSELLING COME IN?

Many mental health problems have their origins in childhood experiences. It is, for example, not difficult to see that bullying at school, bereavement, missing school through illness and so on can be distressing and can, if not addressed at the time, cause problems that last into or resurface in adulthood. Of course the fact that such issues will affect school work will have a lasting effect simply in terms of opportunities in life. But unresolved emotional problems in childhood also have a tendency to affect you as you get older. Problems in childhood can lead to a huge loss of opportunity and missed potential as adults, which is why school-based counselling is seen as increasingly important, and hence this book.

USING THE GLOSSARY

You may have already noticed that some words in this introduction are set in SMALL CAPITALS. This indicates that the glossary on page 83 carries a brief definition and explanation of the term. The SMALL CAPITALS will be used throughout the rest of the book where we feel some explanation might be useful to the reader.

1

SCHOOL-BASED COUNSELLING

IN THE UK

This primer is a brief introduction to school-based counselling across all four UK countries, written for counsellors, trainee counsellors and other interested readers. It will cover primary and secondary school counselling but will focus more on the latter, mainly because this sector has been more extensively researched.

The primer draws mainly on my doctoral research into the effectiveness, processes and outcomes of school-based counselling, and my experience as a researcher and counsellor in various secondary schools in Glasgow.

First, to clarify the definition of school-based counselling: this is one-to-one counselling for school pupils offered by a trained professional and taking place on school premises but organisationally independent of the school and the education system.

Next, a brief history. Counselling in UK secondary schools first emerged in the 1960s, when the Ministry of Education published the Newsom report (Central Advisory Council for Education (England), 1963) recommending that school counsellors should be appointed to help improve low educational attainment. This was followed in 1965 with the launch of the first university courses to train people with teaching experience as school counsellors. By the mid-1970s the training had expanded to include people without teaching experience, and courses now also covered counselling in further and higher education (Baginsky, 2004). Counselling provision in educational settings from secondary schools through to universities increased steadily up until the 1980s. There then followed a sharp decline, broken by a resurgence in the 1990s. Primary school counselling services have been, and continue to be, less widespread, but are increasing, mainly due to the efforts of the charity Place2Be, which was founded in the 1990s, and is currently active in some 235 schools (mostly primary) in England, Wales and Scotland.

School-based counselling is one of the main sources of emotional and psychological support for children and young people in the UK today. About the same number of children and young people have counselling at school as are referred to Child and Adolescent Mental Health Services (CAMHS) (Cooper, 2013). It is one of the most accessible forms of professional emotional support for children and young people in the UK, for two reasons: first, school-based counselling is free at the point of access. Most counsellors in the UK work in private practice, making access more difficult for people who cannot afford to pay. State-funded and voluntary sector counselling services, where they exist, tend to offer counselling only for specific problems (eg. drug and alcohol problems). It can also be hard for people without private transport – and particularly children and young people, who tend to be dependent on an adult for transport – to access counselling services in the community. Publicity can also be a problem: voluntary sector services may not have the resources to market themselves to all age ranges. In schools, counselling services are immediately accessible to pupils, although there may be issues around how the service is presented within the culture of the school. At the same time, it is important to note that some of the most vulnerable young people in the UK may not attend school (for example, homeless young people), so school-based counselling will not be of help to them when seeking support.

Second, seeing a counsellor at school does not involve contact with the psychiatric system nor, importantly, being diagnosed with a mental illness. For many young people, getting help for emotional distress means having to be assessed by a mental health professional first, and deemed mentally ill. There are other sources where you can find out more about the politics of mental health diagnosis (eg. Rapley, Moncrieff & Dillon, 2011; Johnstone, 2014), but we know that young people in particular tend to resist this stigma (Biddle et al, 2007) and there is evidence that it can be harmful to them at this crucial point in their lives where they are developing an identity (Wisdom & Green, 2004).

Adolescence is a time of striving to understand oneself, of experimenting with identities and navigating often powerful pressures to conform. Emotional distress is not uncommon in young people, but framing this as a medical issue can send the message that there is something intrinsically wrong with the person that needs to be fixed. It risks attaching a label and a deficit identity to a young person that they may hold onto, in the absence of any meaningful alternative. Counselling offers them a non-medical space to explore the circumstances that have contributed to their distress and help them move forward, without being labelled mentally ill.

The difference between school-based counselling and mental health care is also a matter of perception. Because it is outside of the MEDICAL MODEL, counselling is often seen as more suitable for lower levels of distress than, say, the psychological services offered in CAMHS, which are seen as dealing with more severe problems. However, research tells us that young people who use their school-based counselling service have similar levels of distress to their peers who are treated within CAMHS (Cooper, 2013). I would argue that school-based counselling is a non-stigmatising and widely accessible source of professional support for children and young people along the spectrum of mental distress.

That said, not all school-age children and young people in the UK have access to a school-based counselling service, and the situation varies from country to country. In Wales, the Assembly Government made it compulsory in 2008 for all secondary schools to offer an independent counselling service to their pupils. This came about following allegations of sexual abuse by a teacher in a Welsh school, and the resulting Children's Commissioner for Wales's *Clywch Inquiry Report* (2004). Based on a thorough review of the evidence, the inquiry concluded that, as teachers are in a position of authority over their pupils, there is a need for adults who are independent of the education system to provide dedicated emotional support in schools. Among the report's recommendations was 'a national strategy for the provision of an independent children's counselling service for children and young people in education' (p.180). An evaluation of the first three years of the Welsh school counselling strategy was published by The British Association for Counselling and Psychotherapy (BACP) and the University of Strathclyde, which showed that counselling was effective, led to a range of improvements and reduced the workload of school staff (Hill et al, 2011). A report from the Welsh Assembly Government in 2016 found that 89 per cent of the 11,567 children and young people receiving independent counselling through their school in 2014/15 did not need to be referred on, and only four per cent were referred to CAMHS (Statistics for Wales, 2016).

In Northern Ireland too, school-based counselling is universal in post-primary and secondary schools. However, in England and Scotland it is left to individual schools to decide if they wish to pay for counselling services for pupils, out of their own budgets; provision varies school by school and there is no national policy, despite openly declared support in principle across all major political parties. Recent estimates indicate that a majority– between 61 and 85 per cent – of secondary schools in England and Scotland (Hanley et al, 2012) do have a counselling service. The statistic is imprecise as the percentage was estimated from the responses to a survey of all secondary schools in Scotland and England. In other words, in 15–39 per cent of secondary schools in Scotland and England, we do not know whether or not there is counselling provision for pupils.

Methodological issues aside, my own experience of working in secondary schools in socially disadvantaged areas of Glasgow has been that provision of a counselling service for pupils is often temporary, because there are too many competing demands on the school budget. So, while the majority of school pupils may have access to a counselling service, it might not always be a secure resource, and children and young people in socially disadvantaged areas (who we know are more likely to experience distress (eg. Myers, McCollam & Woodhouse, 2005)) are least likely to have the option of school-based counselling.

Distress levels among children and young people are high internationally, and the UK is no exception. Suicide among young people is a big problem worldwide. A review of data from 90 countries found that suicide is the fourth most common cause of death for young men aged 15 to 19 and the third for young women in the same age group (Wasserman, Cheng & Jiang, 2005). The same study reported that in most countries suicide rates are actually higher among males than females, and incidence of suicide among young males appears to have increased. Depression has been identified as a risk factor for suicide, and some research shows that it tends to begin most often in adolescence (Brent et al, 1993; Weissman et al, 1999). In fact, about half of all mental health problems are thought to begin before the age of 14, and 75 per cent by the age of 18 (Belfer, 2008; Kessler et al, 2005; Murphy & Fonagy, 2013).

Clearly, distress at a young age can have serious implications for an individual throughout their life. These problems often stay with a person into adulthood (Geller et al, 2001). To understand the impact of this on a person's life, it is also important to remember how closely entwined physical and mental health can be, and research data back this up. Mental health problems in childhood and adolescence have been linked to physical health problems in later life (Goodwin, Davidson & Keyes, 2009), including cardiovascular disease, which is the leading cause of death globally (WHO, 2014). Data like these relate only to diagnosed mental health problems, so the true scale of the problem is likely to be even bigger if you take into account children and young people who are living with undiagnosed serious distress.

The UK Children and Young People's Mental Health and Wellbeing Task Force was set up with government funding in September 2014 to address this issue. The aim of the task force was to investigate and implement improvements to the children and young people's mental health system by consulting with young service users, their parents and carers, and professionals, and by reviewing existing data and previous reports. Its report, *Future in Mind* (Department of Health/NHS England,

2015), summarised the key themes as 'promoting resilience, prevention and early intervention; improving access to effective support – a system without tiers; care for the most vulnerable; accountability and transparency, and developing the workforce' (p.13). It highlights these as areas for improvement and makes recommendations for better provision of mental health services for children and young people in the future. Some of the key recommendations in the report include reducing waiting times for treatment, extending training programmes for CAMHS staff, linking services by removing artificial barriers between them, and sustaining continuous evidence-based improvement.

Schools are expected to take a central role in promoting mental health and providing services for children and young people. Every school is now expected to have a named CAMHS contact and to have developed a 'whole school' approach to promoting pupils' resilience (that is, involving all aspects of the school, from the people in charge of school meals through to senior teaching staff, and including pupils and their parents). Within this framework, counselling is seen as one of the resources that can help children and young people in distress, and in 2016 the Department for Education published *Counselling in Schools: a blueprint for the future,* asserting the 'strong expectation' that all schools make counselling available to pupils. So, the scale of distress experienced by children and young people and the need to improve how we as a society address this has been recognised. Progress is undoubtedly being made in terms of how well education and health services support young people who are in distress or otherwise vulnerable.

One criticism of these documents is that social inequality has been overlooked. In theory, giving schools the freedom to decide for themselves how best to promote the wellbeing of their pupils sounds positive, but this assumes an equal playing field across all schools in all areas and regions. Risks to pupil wellbeing and demands on a school budget are far greater in schools serving areas of social disadvantage. For example, life expectancy for men in Glasgow is more than seven years less than in its neighbouring region East Dunbartonshire (National

Records of Scotland, 2015). Social and economic inequalities have a major influence on how well schools can support individual children and young people, and at the moment this is not adequately recognised in policy.

Having said this, the potential contribution of school-based counselling to improving the wellbeing of children and young people is being highlighted at national policy-making levels, and this is a positive step. Whether the provision of school-based counselling services will actually increase as a result remains to be seen.

2

SCHOOL-BASED COUNSELLING
IN PRACTICE

This chapter gives an overview of the model of school-based counselling as it is commonly practised in the UK today. Worldwide, school-based counselling is well established in 23 countries, and statutory in 37 countries, 32 American states, one Australian state and two Canadian provinces (Harris, 2013). The type or modality of counselling offered varies from country to country. In the US, schools tend to focus on career guidance, but may also offer group-based therapy, usually informed by COGNITIVE BEHAVIOURAL THERAPY (CBT) (Baskin et al, 2010; Dimmitt, Carey & Hatch, 2007; Cooper, 2013). In the UK, school-based counselling more typically offers one-to-one therapy sessions with a focus on emotional support (Cooper, 2009). The model most commonly used is humanistic (Hill et al, 2011; Cooper, 2013), and frequently PERSON-CENTRED.

The humanistic model dates back to the1950s. It contrasts with more established approaches like PSYCHOANALYSIS (most commonly associated with Sigmund Freud) and BEHAVIOURISM (which led to the development of CBT), which tend to view distressed people as damaged in some way and focus on how 'expert' therapists can undo this damage and return the person to psychological health. These theories view a person's distress as a problem that can be treated separately from the rest of their existence, using specific INTERVENTIONS.

HUMANISTIC PSYCHOLOGY tends to view a person's distress as an integral part of who they are, and to take a more holistic approach to understanding their experience and how it might influence their mental/emotional wellbeing.

Humanistic thinking is rooted in EXISTENTIAL philosophy and was applied to psychology by Carl Rogers when he developed client-centred therapy (1951; 1957; 1959), which evolved into PERSON-CENTRED counselling. The person-centred approach is just one of a number of one-to-one therapies that come under the humanistic umbrella, which also embraces POSITIVE PSYCHOLOGY, EXISTENTIAL counselling and GESTALT THERAPY. Broadly, what these different forms of humanistic therapy share is that they regard human beings as self-aware, social, creative and empathic individuals who are geared towards growth and SELF-ACTUALISATION. Human beings in distress cannot be reprogrammed like a machine that has malfunctioned. A person whose life experience has damaged them cannot be repaired like a broken piece of furniture. And a person's unique way of understanding their experience of the world cannot be judged and corrected by an expert therapist. Instead, HUMANISTIC PSYCHOLOGY aims to understand people and their experiences on their own terms, unique to them.

How then does this translate into PERSON-CENTRED practice? You can find a comprehensive overview of person-centred counselling in an earlier book in this series, *The Person-Centred Counselling Primer* (Sanders, 2006). I will give only a brief summary here.

In person-centred counselling the therapy arises from the relationship itself, as opposed to any specific, pre-determined technique that the counsellor applies. The person-centred counsellor aims to meet the client as an equal, not as an 'expert'. The qualities that a person-centred counsellor aims to embody are generally described as the 'CORE CONDITIONS', which Rogers (1957) proposed as 'necessary and sufficient' to promote therapeutic change:

1. Two persons are in psychological contact.
2. The first, whom we shall term the client, is in a state of incongruence, being vulnerable or anxious.
3. The second person, whom we shall term the therapist, is congruent or integrated in the relationship.
4. The therapist experiences unconditional positive regard for the client.
5. The therapist experiences an empathic understanding of the client's internal frame of reference and endeavors to communicate this experience to the client.

6.   The communication to the client of the therapist's empathic understanding and unconditional positive regard is to a minimal degree achieved (p.95).

The conditions relating to the experience of the counsellor (the third, fourth and fifth on Rogers' list) are the cornerstones of person-centred counselling: EMPATHY, UNCONDITIONAL POSITIVE REGARD and CONGRUENCE. Commentators have frequently noted that these three conditions are so fundamentally linked that they may be more usefully thought of as one way of being. Importantly, person-centred counsellors focus on this way of being as opposed to emphasising what the counsellor specifically does. The essential task of a person-centred counsellor is to embody these attitudes in a relationship with the client. In other words, the counsellor understands the client on a deep level, is non-judgmental, and is fully genuine in the relationship. This is a key difference between PERSON-CENTRED therapy and CBT, where specific activities are recommended for specific problems. Person-centred counselling does not seek to 'fix' problems with a view to returning the client to a previous problem-free state. Instead, therapy is seen as a healing process that can be experienced and used by the client in their own unique and unpredictable way.

The remaining two conditions (the second and sixth) relate to the client's experience. Rogers uses the term incongruent to describe the client's condition when they first seek help: that is, in some way distressed, vulnerable or anxious. In practice, the states of CONGRUENCE and incongruence are not black and white – no one is entirely congruent or entirely incongruent, and that includes the counsellor. It may be more useful to think that the counsellor should be the more congruent of the two in the counselling relationship, at least in relation to the client's specific problem that they are bringing to the session. The final condition is that the client actually experiences EMPATHY, UNCONDITIONAL POSITIVE REGARD and CONGRUENCE from the counsellor; it is not enough for the counsellor to experience these attitudes; they must communicate them to the client.

In the UK, a set of competences has been developed that describes the skills, abilities and personal qualities a counsellor practising humanistic therapy should have (Roth, Hill & Pilling, 2009). More recently competences have also been developed for humanistic counselling with children and young people, and specifically those of secondary school age (Hill, Roth & Cooper, 2014). This standardising, or MANUALISING, of humanistic therapy is necessary if researchers are to investigate its effectiveness for reducing distress, and the competences can also be a useful guide or sounding board when training new counsellors or in SUPERVISION of qualified counsellors.

The typical school counsellor will base their approach on the PERSON-CENTRED model, and many will use its theories as a starting point and integrate other forms of therapy. For example, traditionally person-centred counsellors avoid taking an expert role at all, but some routinely use practices that could be seen as DIRECTIVE, and school counsellors who identify with the person-centred approach tend to be in this camp. For instance, it is common for school counsellors to suggest and teach relaxation techniques to young people who may be angry or anxious. Many school counsellors explicitly refer to their practice as 'PERSON-CENTRED/INTEGRATIVE', and they may borrow specific techniques from an approach entirely outside of the humanistic tradition, such as CBT. Alongside, there is a small minority of school counsellors in the UK who identify entirely with a different theoretical orientation, such as CBT or PSYCHODYNAMIC counselling (Hill et al, 2011).

In primary schools, counsellors more commonly offer therapy through 'NON-DIRECTIVE play'. This approach is based on the principles of person-centred counselling, but uses play as the main 'language' of the therapy because young children have limited verbal skills. So the therapy is essentially the same, but the means of communication is slightly different, in order to be age appropriate for younger children. An engaging illustration of non-directive play therapy is given in Virginia Axline's famous book *Dibs in Search of Self* (1964).

Generally, the counselling room in a primary school will contain a wide range of play materials, such as toys, art supplies, games and a sand tray. Young clients are encouraged to explore any of these materials, and counsellors observe their play as an expression of their experience, but without making interpretations or assumptions about the content. For instance, a young client may enact a story using toy figures, and the counsellor may reflect the themes of the story, the feelings of the characters involved, and/or the process of the play, staying within the child's frame of reference. So the child might be playing with a plastic figure of a lion in the sand; the counsellor might describe the child's story thus: 'The lion roared at you, and then you made a sad face,' but not something like 'The lion is angry with you and he reminds you of your dad', which is an interpretation. The counsellor honours the young client's play by witnessing without taking control and, by staying with the child's frame of reference, leaves space for their experience to unfold.

Art and play materials can also be very helpful with older age groups. Counsellors in secondary schools may occasionally use play materials as an alternative to traditional talking therapy, depending on the needs of their young clients. As a secondary school counsellor, I have access to a room full of play materials, and have found that my clients use these in different ways. Some are constantly exploring the play materials to make art, tell stories, invent games etc. David, a 14-year-old pupil with whom I worked, had already repeatedly talked about his experiences to the police and social workers, in a criminal justice process. In the counselling room he wanted to do something different, and spent his time creating, laughing and playing. I was constantly amazed by the power of his imagination, and his ability to find new possibilities every time he entered the counselling room.

Other clients choose to sit down and talk, and show little interest in the art and play materials. When Megan (age 15) started counselling with me, she was ready to talk about her thoughts, her feelings, her experiences and her relationships. She was motivated to communicate with me directly, and chose to do so verbally, ignoring the art and play materials around us.

Sometimes children and young people use art and play materials to alleviate their nerves while they talk. Many young people find it awkward, nerve wracking and overly intense to talk openly to an adult; they prefer to have a distraction. Grant (age 14) would often shuffle playing cards or roll marbles across the table while talking about what was going on in his life. Jenny (age 13) chose to paint while she told me how she felt.

A helpful and comprehensive review of school-based counselling in secondary schools in the UK, including young clients' perceptions and experiences of counselling, was published in 2013 by the University of Strathclyde (Cooper, 2013). The report draws on policy documents, service evaluation reports and published research on school-based counselling, including RANDOMISED CONTROLLED TRIALS (RCTs) to provide an overview of the development, availability, funding, models and OUTCOMES of secondary school-based counselling. It tells us that young people are most commonly referred to a school-based counselling service by pastoral care teachers or other teaching staff, although it is usually possible for pupils to self-refer or for parents to request counselling for their child. The most common issues that bring young people to school-based counselling are family problems and anger, the latter especially so for boys. While the majority of school-based services offer open-ended counselling (ie. there is no limit on the number of sessions), young people actually attend on average between three and six sessions. A large number of clients have just one or two sessions, and a small minority have longer-term therapy. As the therapy progresses, family issues tend to remain prominent, but anger seems to become less of a problem, and issues with self-worth and general relationships tend to emerge. Asked to describe what they hope to gain from counselling (their goals), most young clients say they want to increase their self-confidence and self-acceptance.

So, school-based counselling in the UK is broadly, but not exclusively, person-centred, and art and play materials are commonly used, especially in primary schools. However, there has been relatively little research so far on the actual processes that occur in school-based counselling, and how therapeutic change comes about for children and young people. Chapter 6 reports what I learned from interviews I conducted with a group of secondary school-age young people about their experiences of school-based counselling. Their words give some idea of the change processes that can occur during counselling, but we need to conduct much more research with children and young people, including those of primary school age, if we are to understand more fully how these changes come about.

3

CHILD PROTECTION, CONFIDENTIALITY AND CHILDREN'S RIGHTS

There are particular legal and ethical issues to take into account when providing counselling in schools, and with children and young people more generally, over and above those that apply to work with adults. This chapter gives a brief introduction to some of these legal and ethical aspects of school-based counselling; a full discussion is beyond the scope of this book. You can find a useful and detailed overview of law and policy relating to counselling children and young people in the chapter by Peter Jenkins in the *Handbook of Counselling Children and Young People* (2015). This covers issues such as hierarchy of law, children and young people's legal rights, parents' legal rights, policy and counselling in various contexts, record-keeping and data protection, appearing in court and CONTRACTING.

Another important reference document for all counsellors is the *BACP Ethical Framework for the Counselling Professions* (BACP, 2016). Clause 28 of this framework relates specifically to counselling young people:

> 28. Careful consideration will be given to working with children and young people that:
>
>   a. takes account of their capacity to give informed consent, whether it is appropriate to seek the consent of others who have parental responsibility for the young person, and their best interests.
>
>   b. demonstrates knowledge and skills about ways of working that are appropriate to the young person's maturity and understanding.

CAPACITY TO CONSENT

A key issue in counselling children and young people is whether the young client has the capacity to consent to having counselling in the first place. The younger the client, the less likely they are to have made their own decision about this; counselling in primary schools is most likely to have been arranged between parent(s), teacher(s) and the counsellor. Most young children are assumed not to have the autonomy and maturity to make such decisions about their own wellbeing. As children mature and develop more autonomy they will naturally have more say in deciding whether or not to have counselling. Some secondary school-age young people will make this decision independently of their parents, and this can create a tension that counsellors should be particularly alert to when working with this age group.

In England, Wales and Northern Ireland, the law covering a young person's right to make decisions about their own healthcare needs is based on the 1985 Gillick case.[1] The issue here was whether a doctor could provide contraceptive advice and services to a young person without their parents' knowledge and consent. The court ruled that young people should have the right to access advice and services independently of their parents, provided they are considered to have sufficient maturity and understanding. The Gillick case is relevant to a range of services for young people, including counselling, and young clients are often described as 'Gillick competent' in relation to their capacity to consent.

In Scotland, the law is slightly different, but amounts to the same outcome. The Age of Legal Capacity (Scotland) Act 1991 states that under 16s who are 'capable of understanding the nature and possible consequences' of medical treatments have legal capacity to consent for themselves. Although counselling is not a 'medical treatment' as such, this ruling is widely understood to permit young people under 16 to choose to have counselling without their parents' or legal guardians' consent.

---

1. Gillick vs. West Norfolk Wisbech Area Health Authority [1986] AC 112, [1985] 3 All ER 402, HL.

This is important from a children's rights perspective. Allowing a young person to decide for themselves if they want to have counselling respects their autonomy and right to privacy. However, in practice a young person's right to make their own choice to have counselling is not always borne out, since we know that some 40 per cent of secondary schools require evidence of parental consent before a pupil can access school-based counselling (Jenkins & Polat, 2006). This effectively excludes any young people whose parents do not support their decision to have counselling, or any young people who would prefer not to discuss it with their parents at all. For young people in this position, accessing counselling outside of school can also be difficult, if not impossible. As previously discussed, one of the benefits of a school-based counselling service is its relatively easy access for young people. In practice, most of the young clients I have worked with have discussed counselling with their parents, but a minority have preferred not to, and this is sometimes simply because they don't want their parents to worry about them.

The situation is more complicated when more than one person has legal 'parental responsibility' for the child (Children Act, 1989). Parental consent for a child to have counselling can be given by one parent without the agreement of the other. Obviously both parents' wishes should be taken into account as far as possible, and it is better if all parties are in agreement about a young person's decision to access counselling. But in practice disagreements do arise, particularly where parents are separated or divorced, and counsellors working with children and young people should be prepared for the possibility that a young client may seek their help against a parent's wishes, or without their knowledge. SUPERVISION provides a useful space to reflect on and process this.

CHILD PROTECTION AND CONFIDENTIALITY

Confidentiality is an important part of any counsellor's work, and no less so when working with children and young people.

However, confidentiality in the counselling context is not absolute, even with adult clients. Counsellors routinely discuss the content of sessions with their supervisors, for instance.

The main constraints around client confidentiality when working with children and young people relate to child protection ('safeguarding' in England and Wales) law and policy. School counsellors are not generally required to disclose the content of counselling sessions (McGinnis & Jenkins, 2009) to any other authority unless there are child protection concerns. Child protection is a central concern for any professional working with children and young people.

Counsellors will need to adapt the promise of confidentiality that they offer adult clients to reflect a young client's age, maturity and vulnerability.

The safety of children and young people takes precedence over all other concerns, and school counsellors are required to inform the designated member of staff within the school with responsibility for child protection and safeguarding if they believe any young person is at risk of harm (whether the young person is a client or not). For this reason, it is important to make sure from the outset that the young client understands the limits to confidentiality when they come for counselling and that professionals working with them are required to act to protect them from harm.

In my experience, young people usually disclose risks of harm to an adult (such as a school counsellor) precisely because they want action to be taken. They understand that the counsellor will report the risk and make the decision to share the information on that basis. However, there are also instances when a young client may unintentionally disclose a risk, disclose a risk without considering the implications, or may be unaware of the risk. In those cases, the young person may object to information being shared with anyone else. This situation can be difficult; disclosing information against the client's wishes may undermine the counselling relationship. However, the young person's safety comes before this and any other concerns.

Risk of harm includes instances where a young client discloses suicidal intention or where they are in danger of physical and/or sexual abuse. Although the *legal* duty of a counsellor to report abuse is not as clear cut as it is widely perceived to be (Jenkins & Palmer, 2012), breaching confidentiality to protect children and young people from serious harm is an *ethical* duty, and often a requirement of the school or counselling agency. This is an important issue where there is often some confusion: there is a statutory obligation on local authorities to report suspected child abuse; individual counsellors may be required to report suspected child abuse under their employment terms and conditions, and/or their profession's code of ethics, but not by law.

In situations where there is a clear risk of serious harm, child protection procedures provide the school counsellor with a straightforward course of action. However, where the level of risk is lower, school counsellors are regularly faced with more complex ethical dilemmas. For instance, it is not unusual for young people in secondary school to drink alcohol when they are still below the legal age limit.[2] A school counsellor who knows that a young client is drinking alcohol will have to make their own assessment about the extent of risk of harm to the individual, and balance this against the possible consequences of breaching confidentiality.

Another example is sexual activity. Children under the age of 13 are not deemed legally capable of consenting to sex (Sexual Offences Act, 2003); any disclosures of sexual contact with an adult (aged 16 and over) should be reported as abuse. Regardless of how the young person perceives and describes the relationship, it is sexual abuse. However, a disclosure of consensual sex between two 15-year-olds is a different matter. Although both are below the legal age of consent, treating this as a child protection issue may do more harm than good. In both

---

2. Young people aged under 18 cannot buy or drink alcohol in a public place; young people aged 16–17 can drink beer, wine or cider with a meal in a licensed premises but only if there is an adult present; children and young people aged five to 16 can drink alcohol in their own home or other private premises.

cases, the school counsellor must carefully consider first and foremost how best to protect the young people involved from harm and respect their client's confidentiality as far as possible within those parameters. Again, this is what supervision is for; it ensures counsellors are not working in professional isolation with these ethical dilemmas, and a school counsellor should discuss these decisions with their supervisor.

Some commentators have reported the development recently of a 'reporting culture' in the UK (Jenkins, 2010; Lines, 2010). There is a perception that counsellors and other professionals are becoming less likely to use their discretion and more likely to automatically report any disclosure, in order to avoid personal culpability. This is understandable; adopting a hard and fast rule to report *any* suspicion of *any* level of harm alleviates some of the anxiety over ethical dilemmas. However, there are downsides to this approach. The NSPCC (2008), for example, recognises that the knowledge that a counsellor will immediately report what they say to the authorities may deter some children and young people from sharing information about their abuse, and that abused children may be more likely to seek help when 'they retain some control of the events that directly involve them' (p.32). This is why hotlines like ChildLine (now run by the NSPCC) are so important, as they give children and young people the option to talk to an adult without having to reveal their identity. The NSPCC says there is a need for a 'mixed economy' of services for children and young people, where different levels of confidentiality apply.

EXPLAINING BOUNDARIES

Given the necessary limits to confidentiality in counselling children and young people, how do counsellors make this clear to clients? The counsellor needs to discuss child protection issues and confidentiality openly and clearly at the start, when they first meet a new client, and make sure the young client understands what will happen if they do disclose risk of harm to themselves or another child or young person. This reduces the likelihood that a young client will experience any breach of confidentiality as a breach of trust.

With very young clients, counsellors will need to use age-appropriate language and often non-verbal communication. For primary school children, the BOUNDARIES of confidentiality within the counselling relationship can be communicated using art and play materials. This could take the form of drawing or making a physical piece of work with the young client, and is a good way to help a young client understand ideas that may be beyond their level of verbal development. For the youngest primary school clients, the nuances of confidentiality may be too complex to understand, so the main point to emphasise is that the counsellor will not 'keep secrets'.

Other more everyday aspects of counselling BOUNDARIES can be covered in the same way with young children: for example, drawing a clock to explain when you will meet for sessions and for how long.

Verbal explanations are more likely to be appropriate with secondary school-age children, but don't assume they will be able to read well enough to understand written explanations. Nor can you assume that young people of secondary school age have a full understanding of the issues involved. You may need to explore concepts like confidentiality with the young client to establish exactly what they understand by the term. Let the client know that you want them to be safe. When explaining that you will report child protection concerns, say exactly what will happen – who within the school you will inform, and what they are then likely to do. Giving examples can encourage a discussion.

SUPPORT FOR SCHOOL COUNSELLORS

Working with children and young people presents some tricky ethical, legal and professional dilemmas for counsellors. While in most cases the ethical course of action for a school counsellor is clear, there are also instances where you will have to weigh up conflicting rights, policies and ethical principles.

This is part of the responsibility that counsellors take on when they decide to work with children and young people. It can be a challenging role, and you need to have adequate professional and managerial support.

Ideally, you will be working in an environment where support is readily available from peers and the school staff. But in many cases the counsellor will be working relatively independently within a school. This is not necessarily untenable, provided you have good communication with the school staff responsible for child protection. In either situation, individual supervision is a crucial support, as it is for all counsellors. For this reason it is important that school counsellors work with a supervisor who understands the specific issues relevant to working with these age groups.

4

DIVERSITY, EQUALITY
AND SOCIAL JUSTICE

As previously explained, school-based counselling is widely accessible, but not to all children and young people in the UK. This chapter considers the diversity of needs for counselling among children and young people and the (in)equality of access. It would be impossible in the space of this chapter, or indeed this book, to fully discuss diversity and equality in relation to school-based counselling. It is also unlikely that a counsellor's initial professional training will have addressed the issue in sufficient depth and detail, so I encourage counsellors working in schools, and trainees, to assess their own development needs in relation to these issues and seek out further reading and training courses as they think necessary. A good starting point would be *Anti-Discriminatory Practice in Counselling and Psychotherapy*, edited by Colin Lago and Barbara Smith (2010).

This chapter will give a broad overview of some of the issues school-based counsellors might consider in relation to diversity, anti-discrimination and equality.

Counselling and diversity

As discussed, school-based counsellors in the UK mostly use a PERSON-CENTRED or broadly HUMANISTIC approach. One criticism of this approach relates to its theoretical focus on the client as an individual, without reference to their social context. For example, social issues like poverty and racism are not taken into consideration. Person-centred theory is not unusual in this regard, and any one-size-fits-all theory of counselling can overlook important aspects of a client's experience, and particularly their experience of cultural identity and social inequality. It is worth remembering that most counselling theory and practice originated in European and/or North American psychology. For this reason, counselling itself is built on a set of constructs that are steeped in white, male, able-bodied, heterosexual, American/Eurocentric culture. Issues of social class and opportunity are not acknowledged either.

As Lago (2007; 2011) discusses in detail, even the terms 'difference' and 'diversity' are defined against the dominant culture. In other words, certain privileged categories in society are deemed 'normal' and taken for granted as the counterpoint to what is 'different'. For example, in Western society white people are considered the default race. This means that white racial identity is effectively ignored, and the power and privilege that comes with it are therefore obscured. This obscuring works to disadvantage non-white people. The same mechanisms are at play for other disadvantaged groups, including women, disabled people and lesbian, gay, bisexual and transgender (LGBT) people. In the counsellor–client relationship there is a danger that, by ignoring cultural differences, we collude with this structural inequality.

YOUNG PEOPLE AS A DISADVANTAGED GROUP

Lago (2007) includes young people on a list of disadvantaged groups, arguing that they are seen as different from the norm, which would be people of working age. This reflects the common representation of young people in the media as 'feral youth'. So, a young client's age is in itself something that influences their social status. Adolescence is a time of developing an independent identity, and how a young person is seen by and in relation to others is highly significant. With this in mind, school counsellors should be aware of the power imbalance that exists between an adult professional and a young client. In my experience, adults working with adolescents can often underestimate this, and overlook the young person's tendency to defer to them. Adulthood tends to come with a gradual and sometimes subtle increase in confidence, and it is easy for an adult to see young people as more powerful than they may in fact feel.

Consider how a young client navigates their developing identity. How do they see themselves in relation to their peers, or in relation to adults? How do they balance a growing sense of independence and autonomy with (usually) financial and practical dependence on others? People learn about themselves primarily through their relationships to others, and moving from childhood to adulthood brings significant changes in these dynamics with parents, other relatives, peers and teachers.

DIVERSITY AMONG YOUNG CLIENTS

Many children and young people accessing school-based counselling belong to a specific disadvantaged group that is an important part of their identity. School counsellors will need to sensitise themselves to their client's particular experience, which is often one of social marginalisation, in order to build a therapeutic relationship. Both research and experience suggest that aiming to treat all clients in the same way and simply ignoring cultural differences does not meet the needs of all clients. How can someone feel fully understood in a relationship where part of their identity is ignored?

For example, research (here in relation to adult clients) has found that 'race-avoidant' white therapists tend to have shorter and less successful relationships with their black clients than do white therapists who are comfortable with openly acknowledging the difference (Thompson & Jenal, 1994). As a step towards working therapeutically with a wider range of clients, school counsellors can start by exploring their own cultural identities and the power they have, or do not have, in society as a whole. In other words, counsellors can move towards a more inclusive way of working if they first 'check their privilege' (Freeman, 2013). This term, now widely used in social media, in essence asks people to take into account the ways in which they are advantaged by belonging to particular social groups.

For example, I find it important to reflect on the ways in which being white, able-bodied, heterosexual and university educated has conferred social advantages in my life, whether I am aware of it or not. This kind of reflection can often be painful. It is far more comfortable to focus on our triumphs over adversity than to examine the unfair advantages we have over others. Accepting that you hold a privileged social position means to some extent letting go of such psychological bedrock beliefs as 'life is fair'. You may have heard of the 'just-world effect' – a concept that social psychologists have used since the 1960s. It describes our profound need to believe that the world is inherently fair. Of course, this is understandable, and serves a protective purpose. The bad news is that holding the belief that life is fair appears to reduce our ability to empathise with those whose lives are manifestly marked by unfairness. It encourages us to believe that unfairness only happens to bad people. This is the psychological root of 'victim blaming'; we assign responsibility for crime or injustice to the people who have been hurt by it. The same bias in thinking makes it difficult for us to understand our own, individual social privilege.

Counsellors have a responsibility to explore for themselves the advantages they may have had, and to question their assumptions about fairness. I mention this particularly because there is evidence to suggest that the counselling community as a whole needs to improve its cultural sensitivity. For example, another study has found that white counselling trainees rarely explore their attitudes to ethnic identity (Dhillon-Stevens, 2004). Conversely, non-white counselling trainees can feel silenced in environments where race is not discussed openly (Ellis & Cooper, 2013; Watson, 2006). So, white counsellors may tend towards being race avoidant, at least in their initial training, and this perpetuates white privilege in counselling training.

What could this mean for young clients from black and minority ethnic (BME) backgrounds? Does school-based counselling adequately meet their needs? BME young people, and especially Asian young people, are under-represented in UK school-based counselling (Cooper, 2013). Interestingly, this is not the case when school-based counselling services are offered online (Hill et al, 2011). So what makes BME young people less likely to access school-based counselling services? And what is it about online counselling that reverses this tendency? School counsellors (especially white school counsellors) may want to reflect on these questions and consider the particular needs of BME children and young people. This is a question of ethical practice, since not acknowledging the identity development of a young person from a minority group can disadvantage them in later life (Smith & Widdowson, 2003; Charura, 2012). This applies across a range of difference and diversity issues.

GREATER VULNERABILITY TO DISTRESS AMONG MINORITY GROUPS

Belonging to a minority group within a majority culture tends to make people more vulnerable to distress. Higher levels of mental health problems are reported for people from various disadvantaged groups – for example, those with learning disabilities (Raghavan & Patel, 2005). However, it is also important to note that there is evidence of prejudice in mental health diagnosis; people who differ from the dominant social norm are more likely to be given a diagnosis of mental disorder (Read, 2004). This gives an indication of the pervasiveness of oppression and discrimination, and the need to be proactive in working against it.

In a school context, young people who are considered different in some way may be more vulnerable to bullying and may suffer the psychological consequences of that. For instance, homophobic and transphobic bullying is rife in schools (Guasp, 2012; Russell et al, 2011), so young people starting the process of understanding their own gender and sexual identity will already have been exposed to prejudice. The impact of this on distress levels is considerable – we know, for example, that LGBT young people are more likely to consider and attempt suicide (Suicide Prevention Resource Center, 2008; Fergusson, Horwood & Beautrais, 1999; Grossman & D'Augeli, 2007).

Besides bullying, there are other issues relating to cultural difference that counsellors may not have considered. Disabled children are significantly more likely to experience abuse and maltreatment, and this appears to be underestimated by professionals and policy-makers (Stalker & McArthur, 2012). If school-based counselling services are to provide support for disabled children and young people, careful thought and planning is needed for specific impairments. For instance, in their chapter on diversity in *The Handbook of Counselling Children and Young People*, Pattison, Charura and McAndrew (2015) discuss ways of overcoming communication barriers when counselling deaf children and young people. Their recommendations demonstrate the level of proactive work needed if counsellors want to offer a truly inclusive service.

A NOTE ON GENDER NORMS

Gender is a powerful example of the way social identity issues can be a source of young people's distress. Historically, women have been subject to prejudice in mental health diagnosis (Read, 2004), and structural inequalities continue to disadvantage women in many ways, including greater vulnerability to physical and sexual violence. Young women are more likely than young men to self-harm, to develop eating disorders, and to attempt suicide. At the same time, distress among young men is also a serious problem, and they are actually more likely to complete suicide. For transgender young people, suicide and self-harm are even more likely than for those who identify with the gender they were assigned at birth (known as being *cis*gender). All young people, as they begin to understand themselves as individuals, are under pressure from strict gender norms to behave in certain ways, and those who do not conform are often stigmatised, discriminated against, and treated harshly. Transgender young people face the worst of this, but there are myriad ways in which a young person may not fit the social role that they are expected to play, and may suffer as a result. For instance, girls and boys are often judged by the dominance of their behaviour: girls are referred to as 'bossy' for the same behaviour that is expected (or, indeed, demanded) from boys.

A key example of a dangerous cultural message about gender is that men and boys are discouraged from crying, or from expressing emotion generally. This works to isolate men and boys from their support networks when they are in distress, creating a barrier to seeking help that may contribute to a higher risk of suicide for men, and especially for young men. This is linked to homophobia and transphobia. Boys and young men are judged against a one-dimensional macho stereotype and often derided as 'gay' for stepping outside of it, regardless of their sexual orientation. Gender norms, and the way in which they are upheld in schools and communities, are damaging across the board.

For girls and young women, seeking help appears to be somewhat easier, but distress is still widespread. A large proportion of young people are sexually active, and the rate of school-age pregnancies is higher in the UK than anywhere else in Europe. Girls and young women are vulnerable to double standards in relation to their developing sexuality: they experience pressure to engage in sex, yet are stigmatised if and when they do – and they are, of course, at greater biological risk (ie. unwanted pregnancy) than their male peers. Women and girls are more likely to experience physical and sexual violence, and cultural responses to this often tend towards victim-blaming.

In Stuebenville, Ohio in 2012, a 16-year-old girl was sexually assaulted by two young men while she was unconscious. More than a dozen other young people at the party photographed, video-recorded and posted images and film of the assault on social media. The girl was then harassed by members of the community who perceived her to be at fault and to have ruined the promising football careers of the young men who assaulted her. This is an example of victim blaming, within the framework of what is referred to as 'rape culture'.

A bill to introduce compulsory sex and relationship education in schools was recently put forward in the UK parliament, which would have helped young people explore and understand issues around sexual consent. This type of education could be an important antidote to rape culture. However, a majority of MPs voted against this bill and, as a result, many young people in schools are still not adequately prepared for the issues facing them when they become sexually active. Advancing technology adds to this difficulty. Around 15 per cent of 11–16-year-olds have sent, posted online, or received explicit sexual images. Although this can be a normal part of teenage sexual experimentation, it can also be experienced as harmful, and this is more often the case for girls than for boys (Livingstone & Gorzig, 2014).

WHAT CAN A COUNSELLOR DO?

The school counsellor has the complicated task of navigating gender identity and sexuality issues with all young clients while keeping a check on their own assumptions around gender norms. More generally, personal development work across the full range of diversities can help school counsellors to offer a genuinely inclusive service to children and young people and develop their awareness of issues that may make it more difficult for clients to access school-based counselling. For instance, did any part of this chapter make you feel defensive? If so, why and how? Have these issues been touched on by your young clients? In what way? How have you responded? Personal development work and SUPERVISION are vital for counsellors if they are to avoid colluding with social injustices.

What else can we as counsellors do about social injustice? Psychotherapists and Counsellors for Social Responsibility (PCSR) is an organisation for practitioners in these professions who are interested in politics and social responsibility. There are others, some specific to a particular discipline or geographical area. Opportunities to meet and debate with other counsellors and therapists interested in working for social justice are a good way to raise awareness, access peer support and inspiration and generate collective action to bring about change.

5

A SCHOOL-BASED
COUNSELLING SESSION

This is an extract taken from a real school-based counselling session, recorded and transcribed with the client's prior permission, with some details changed to protect his confidentiality. It illustrates a typical exchange between a young client and a school counsellor, who uses a classical person-centred approach in the session. The client was 15 years old at the time, and had been struggling with emotional problems since his mother had a heart attack a few years before.

Key:
T = Therapist
C = Client

T: So how are things this week?

C: Eh... well, it's got a bit worse because it was actually last Friday, me and my mum and dad and my sister... my pals came up and it was about 9 o'clock and my mum came in and she said 'They'll have to go home now', and I said 'Another 10 minutes', and she said 'That's you grounded again', because it was like 15 minutes after she asked us. She said, 'I've asked once, I've asked twice and I'm not asking another time so you're grounded again'. And then I just really went off my nut... I just got really angry when they went, and I pushed my mum into the wall and she fell and I don't know why I did that. I know it was wrong to do that, so I went back in my room and I started screaming. I thought I was taking a panic attack, and I don't know why.

[Here, the client expresses his anger quite strongly, but also his bewilderment about having the feeling and not fully understanding it].

T: You felt kind of out of control?

[The counsellor interjects only briefly, so as not to interrupt the flow of the client's story, and chooses to focus on his reaction to the anger, which is more important in this moment than the anger itself.]

C: Mmhmm, and then my dad came in when I was lying on my bed screaming and he holded me down, and then my mum came in and she holded me down and all, and I kept on saying 'Don't, don't, don't' and she was like 'Don't do what, what are you trying to say?'. I don't know what I was trying to say because I was like a different person.

T: You didn't feel like you.

[Again the counsellor's response is concise, and focuses on the client's experience, not on the specifics of the story he is telling.]

C: Aye, and my dad went into the living room and told my sister and then my mum, I seen her greeting because she didn't want to look at me and that. And then I just went bonkers again, threw a bottle at the door and she was like that, 'What did you do that for?' and then she made me a pizza and she gave me the pizza and I threw the pizza at the wall.

[The client seems agitated as he tells the story, focusing on details and caught up in the anger as he relives this experience.]

T: How did it feel when you were in the middle of that? How did it feel? Just so angry or...?

[The counsellor moves from brief reflections of the experience that the client is describing to a direct question

to facilitate his focusing on the feeling, ie. his anger.]

C: I wasn't like me, it just – it's hard to explain it but… when you – before I do it, it's like it goes into my head and then you just need to like do something to let go of that anger and I just find the closest thing that's near me and then I just do whatever, and that makes me feel better.

[*In answer to the counsellor's question, the client gives more explanation of what happens to him when he feels uncontrollable anger.*]

C: And the only thing I want from my mum, is like… she's really overprotective with me, and I get that because she loves me and I know that, and that's the only thing I want is to be – to have freedom, like to go outside and have peace and everything.

[*Having explained the process of his anger to some extent, the client moves unprompted towards describing some of the feelings underneath the anger.*]

T: It feels like she's not giving you any freedom, and that's the only thing you want.

[*The counsellor turns her attention to the next issue raised by the client – his desire for freedom and feeling that he has none, which moves the session forward.*]

C: I know she's just grounding me because she doesn't want me to go outside and get hurt or anything. I think it's going to be like this all the way until I'm 25 or something. I'll be still living there, like I'll be 18 and she's still doing it.

T: So it feels as if it's not going to change; it's like 'I'm stuck in this situation'.

[Here the counsellor responds to the client's complaint about the future while subtly bringing the focus back to his feeling in the present, of being stuck in a situation that he does not like.]

C: It feels like I'm going to be here forever; it's like a prison or something, like a jail; that's what it feels like and the only peace I get, the freedom I get is going to school. And that's the only thing I want from her. I've asked her that, I just want freedom. My dad understands me because I've talked to him and I said 'The only thing I want is to get out and have a laugh with my pals', and he was like that, 'Aye, I understand you', and I was like that, 'No wonder I'm quite depressed all the time now, because I'm stuck in a dark room', and then he said, 'Your life wasn't like mine when I was young, I used to go out all the time'... I'm dying to get that, dying to just have freedom.

[This allows the client to describe the feeling more vividly – 'like a prison' – and he moves his focus to what he wants, repeatedly using the word 'freedom'.]

T: Just that freedom – let me have a wee bit of freedom.

[The counsellor uses the client's word 'freedom', and chooses to focus on this positive goal rather than the negative feeling associated with it. She also speaks in the first person, which emphasises her focus on his frame of reference.]

C: I've been trying to make her feel sorry for me; I've been like not feeding myself.

[At this stage the client feels comfortable enough to admit to a behaviour that is not necessarily socially acceptable, whereas earlier in the session, describing his angry outburst, he had been apologetic: 'I know it was wrong'.

This suggests he is feeling gradually more secure in the counsellor's acceptance of him.]

T: Kind of deliberately not eating so that she thinks there's something wrong?

[*The counsellor's reaction is non-judgmental. She is checking that she understands what he is saying.*]

C: I actually had a dream that I was punching my mum – she said that I punched her and I didn't, I pushed her, but that was just – that wasn't me, because I would never push her because obviously she had a heart attack and all that. I would never punch her either.

T: It's like when that happens – you've said that a few times, 'It wasn't me'. It's almost like, 'I can see it happening, but it's not me doing it'. It's like… the anger takes over or something.

[*The counsellor stays with the client's frame of reference instead of challenging the inconsistency. She demonstrates that she is not concerned with the external truth of the situation but only with the client's experience. She does not push him to take responsibility for pushing his mum, and reflects his feeling of being out of control of his actions.*]

C: I've tried to explain that to her and said, 'It wasn't me, it was like… I don't know what it was', and she just doesn't believe me; she thinks it's all me, and it's not.

T: So she thinks you deliberately did it but it's like – 'It's not something I would have chosen to do if I was in control of that'.

[*Again, the counsellor frames her response from the client's perspective, speaking here (and elsewhere) as if in the*

client's voice. She lets him know that she believes him when
he says he did not intend to hurt his mum.]

T: Is that how it feels?

[*She also checks the accuracy of her reflections with the
client, showing her tentativeness in understanding him,
and willingness to be corrected if she is not quite right.*]

T: It's like, 'I didn't want to push you, mum'?

[*Here, instead of using the client's own words, the counsellor
to some extent translates what he is saying: his conflict
between having pushed his mum and his feeling that this
is not something he would do. She reflects the message she
suspects is underneath: 'I didn't want to push you, mum'.*]

C: I didn't want to push her, it just comes out of me, then it just
fires at the first thing it sees and I just want to know why
I'm doing that and all, because I've never done that before,
I've never hurt my mum.

[*Now the client starts to move towards accepting
responsibility for the action, even though he still finds it
painful to admit and difficult to understand.*]

T: Does that worry you, the fact that you did that?

[*The counsellor tentatively reflects a potential emotion
behind the client's desire to know why he acted this way.*]

C: Aye, when I had that dream that I punched her, it was
like I was turning into pure evil and I woke up sweating.
I don't want that to be me. I'm dead moody in the house
and then even with a disagreement, if I'm disagreeing with
somebody over something stupid, I just get really, really
angry and I never used to be like that.

[*In response to the counsellor's question about 'worry', the client describes his feelings about this, which are stronger than worry and more like fear.*]

T: You don't want that to be you, it's so scary. And it feels like it's – it's like this big evil anger over something kind of stupid?

[*Using the client's words, the counsellor adapts her reflection to the stronger emotion. She also hears and reflects the client's strong word 'evil', while associating it with his anger, slightly separating it from the client himself. While she hears and understands his sense of the 'evil' in hurting his mum, and his fear over what this means, she does not reinforce the fear that he himself is 'evil'.*]

C: I think I wouldn't do it if I got just one day to get freedom because it's just bringing all the anger out, and I think that's why I'm doing it because it's like too much stuff I don't like going on.

[*At this point, the client's words demonstrate his progression from denying the behaviour he does not like or understand to questioning his motives, expressing his fear, and now understanding his behaviour as a response to his stress. This is a more self-accepting attitude, brought about by experiencing the counsellor's acceptance of him.*]

T: It's kind of all building up and building up and then it's just going boom.

C: Even when I try to talk to her about being down, she's like that, 'I don't know, do what you want, everything's up to you remember', and I was like, 'Aye, but I want advice off you, what would you do?' and she was like that, 'Well I don't have the problems you do', and I don't have any problems. I don't like that. I remember I was looking at photos from when I was wee and she looked – every picture was me and her, me and her, and it used to be like that. She used to love me, all the time she used to be with me all the time, and every Saturday she used to take me out to a shop I would want to go to and on Saturday there she was like, 'I've no money to buy you stuff' and I said, 'I don't want stuff, I don't want anything off you, I just want love and peace and freedom off people, I don't want anything bought for me'.

[The client now moves on to talk about missing his previous warmer relationship with his mum.]

T: It's like, 'I don't want any material stuff, I don't want things; I want attention, I want love'. You mentioned that a couple of times about love, when you were saying how different things were before, you said, 'She used to love me all the time,' and then again you said, 'I just want love'. Does it feel as if you're not getting that from her, you're not getting love from her?

[Having reflected and summarised important elements of the client's experience and taken time to emphasise his desire for his mum's love, the counsellor then focuses this into a question about how he feels about the relationship now.]

C: I'm not getting anything from her; it's like I'm not there. When I'm talking to her, it's like I'm not there, she can't hear me, and I want her to like love me and cherish me and all that.

[Gradually, the client goes deeper into the complex feelings behind his anger, expressing hurt about feeling ignored and unloved. The counsellor's responding from his frame of reference allows him to follow this process through.]

T: And it doesn't feel like that just now.

[In any session, the counsellor is unlikely to respond to every important part of what is said, and in this instance the counsellor omits the client's feelings of being ignored and unloved, though she has referenced both of these feelings earlier in the session.]

C: I want to know why she's like ignoring me all the time and I've asked her that. I've said, 'Why are you ignoring me? Why do you not love me?' And she's like, 'Oh shut up, I do love you and I don't ignore you'. But she does; I can see it, because I want to have all the conversation I can get with her before – because I know, I know for a fact there's going to be another heart attack coming because she's smoking again. It was partly the smoking and now she's smoking again and I feel like I've just got a wee bit of time left before she has another heart attack.

[The client then repeats the part of his experience that the counsellor had not reflected back to him – the feeling of being ignored and unloved – demonstrating that it is important for him to have this acknowledged. He goes on to reveal more of the deep feelings behind his anger, this time his fear of losing his mum.]

T: It's like, 'I don't know how long we have', and it feels as if it's precious time, and you want her attention.

[The counsellor's brief response includes reference to the emotion she had previously missed – 'You want her attention' – as well as his newly expressed fear, 'I don't know how long we have'.]

C: That's why I was trying to talk to her, because she needs to talk to me now. I don't want to say like, 'You're going to have another heart attack,' but I've just got a feeling she's going to have another one. Like a gut feeling.

[*The client expresses a sense of urgency about changing his relationship with his mum, showing some of the trauma he experienced from her previous heart attack.*]

T: That's why you want her to talk to you now.

C: I can see it in my head and I just don't want her to be like this all the time, because if it does happen, I'm never going to get that love from her.

T: It's like it'll be too late, it's like – 'I want you now, I want your love now, I want your attention, I want that relationship now'.

[*The counsellor's words match the client's intensity and sense of urgency. She does not minimise his fear or attempt to pacify him.*]

C: I just want everything to change, just everything, like everything. When my mum had the heart attack it's like I can't leave the house; I need to be there with her in case something happens; I'm constantly worrying and worrying about her, like if I go out somewhere I can't have a good time because I'm constantly worrying and saying, 'What if my mum is like collapsed or something the now, and I'm not there? I need to be there when it happens'.

T: So there's something about you feeling like a prisoner, but then there's also that bit of you that actually has to be there, and when you're out it's like your mind is there, 'What if something happens to her?'.

[*This response from the counsellor demonstrates complexity in reflecting different feelings about going out that the client describes at different points in the session, ending with the most pertinent one in the moment.*]

C: I just want everything to change really.

T: You want to change it all.

[*Here the counsellor paraphrases the client, but in a way that puts more emphasis on his agency in the situation.*]

C: I want it to be like it used to be when I was a wean. I know this heart – well, I hope it doesn't come, but I know it's going to come because she's smoking one fag after the other and I know it's going to come and she's coughing her guts up in the morning… I thought, it sounds like she's dying when she's coughing. So I just want to get it all right before it does happen.

T: So it sounds as if you're trying to say, 'I want it to be different, I want it to be back that way', and there's this big pressure on you that's a big pressure, 'I need to get this sorted now'.

[*The counsellor links the client's themes of wanting to change everything and feeling urgency in his relationship with his mum, and notes that this is creating stress for him.*]

C: My sister, she said to me, 'If you give your mum time, and you be nice, you go to school, then you'll probably get what you want'. I just want them to understand, but they just don't – and they think I need help. It's like I want them to get help... when you think about it, it's her that's making me depressed. I don't mean that in a bad way, it's not her.

[*At this point, and earlier in the session, the client protests about the way other people are trying to locate the problem with him, showing a fuller understanding of his emotions in context. He wants his feelings to be accepted as an understandable response to the stresses he is experiencing and not considered abnormal.*]

T: But it's like living in this situation, this is what's pulling me down; this is what's making me feel this way; this is what's making me angry. If this was all sorted, I'd feel better.

[*The counsellor comes back to the bigger picture of understanding the client's anger, the issue he began the session with, and reflects in an encouraging way his developing perspective on how he's feeling, emphasising the reason behind it. This response implicitly rejects the pathologising attitude which he is protesting against. She is implicitly reassuring him that she does not believe he will always feel this way, or that there is something wrong with him. She is accepting his perspective that living in his current situation is hard for him and provokes some difficult emotions. She also directs her response to the possibility of a better future: 'If this was all sorted, I'd feel better'. This is a very supportive response for this client, who seems to feel disempowered and insulted by the suggestion that there is something wrong with him.*]

This extract is presented here to illustrate a real school-based counselling session using a PERSON-CENTRED approach. It shows how a young client can move towards accepting difficult experiences by meeting acceptance from the counsellor. This counsellor creates a safe space for the client, respecting his feelings and staying within his frame of reference. She does not make judgments about his feelings or his actions. She does not investigate the truth of his account to establish what 'really' happened. She does not make interpretations about deeper feelings beneath what he is telling her. Instead she gently and skillfully allows him to work at his own pace, supported by her EMPATHY and acceptance, while he reaches his own conclusions. This is not a rigid prescription for how school-based counselling should be; it is simply one example of a helpful session. The next chapter describes other processes that may be helpful in school-based counselling.

6

CHANGE PROCESSES IN
SCHOOL-BASED COUNSELLING

It seems self-evident that people benefit from talking about their emotions. Most people will have had the experience of feeling better about a problem after speaking to someone about it. All counselling relies on this basic premise that talking to a 'good listener' can be helpful to people if they are distressed or trying to deal with a problem in life. When young people are asked what they find helpful about their counselling, the most common response is 'The opportunity to talk to someone who listens' (Cooper, 2013), or some variant of that.

But how exactly does talking to someone who is listening translate into feeling better? What are the stages between opening up about your emotions and making a positive change in your life? I attempted to address these questions about school-based counselling as part of my PhD, and the change processes I describe in this chapter are based on some of my findings (McArthur, Cooper & Berdondini, 2015). I interviewed 14 clients aged 13–16 about their experiences of school-based counselling and analysed their descriptions in order to identify the possible processes of change that can occur for young people. The young people's names have been changed to protect their confidentiality but the quotes are taken directly from the interviews. I have also given each young person's age at the time of the counselling.

Five distinct pathways of change emerged from what the young people said about the impact of talking about their emotions with a counsellor at school. Some talked about just one process, but most of them described a number of different processes that overlapped or occurred simultaneously. Young people reached similar outcomes by different means. For example, most of them experienced an improvement in their relationships but for some this came about because they felt less angry, while for others it seemed to be linked to having more self-esteem. Often a positive change in one area of a young person's life could snowball and lead to further positive changes in other areas.

So it seems that there is more than one answer to the question of how talking to a counsellor might help people, and a client is likely to experience more than just one process of change. Each person's process in counselling is unique and complex, and you could argue that there are as many pathways to change as there are clients. The change processes described here are broad categorisations that summarise the experiences of a small group of young people. They are presented here as examples of potential pathways to change for young people in school-based counselling, not as an exhaustive list.

RELIEF

The change process most often described by these young people was one where talking about their emotions gave them some relief, or made them feel less burdened, which reduced the effects of their negative emotions. In other words, counselling functioned as *catharsis*, and talking about emotions took some of the pressure off young people who were struggling to cope. They found that through talking they became less worried and less angry. Some of their statements about counselling revealed this process:

> When you've spoke about it you feel better because you've finally got it out and told someone how you feel (Hannah, age 13).

Having some relief from their emotions then led to other changes in their lives. Young people found they were better able to focus and concentrate at school, which improved their school work. Stress and negative emotions can be a powerful distraction, and when young people are distressed it can be incredibly difficult to cope with school work. It stands to reason that feeling relieved of negative emotions may make it easier for young people to concentrate, and this has been suggested by research on school-based counselling too (eg. Rupani, Haughey & Cooper, 2012). For other young people, talking about anger and then feeling less angry meant that their behaviour towards other people changed. Once they were less likely to act aggressively towards their friends and peers, their relationships with them improved too:

> I got to talk about my anger... now I've not been angry with anybody. I'm not getting suspended and all that any more... because I'm not fighting (Josh, age 13).

Not only were Josh's negative emotions a distraction from his schoolwork; his anger had also meant he sometimes missed school, and having some relief from the anger meant that this was less likely to happen.

For some of the young people, the process of relief and having more manageable emotions meant that they were able to sleep better:

> I'm happier to go to bed... it's easier to relax and, I don't know, it feels like I'm not as worried (Chloe, age 16).

It is easy to imagine how the positive outcomes associated with this process of talking about their problems and feeling relief – sleeping well, doing well at school and enjoying better relationships with others – could feed back into a virtuous cycle of feeling better.

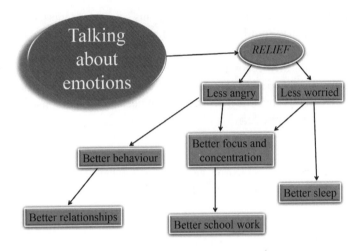

SELF-WORTH

Importantly, what the young person says is only part of the story. The counsellor's response to them is crucial, as the young people emphasised when describing another process of change – that of increasing self-worth. In this process, talking about their emotions was met with the counsellor's listening, understanding, accepting and valuing of them. Stuart (age 16) said, 'She didn't judge me, and listened to what I had to say'. Rachel (age 14) described the counsellor as 'someone who listens to me and [...] like understands, and doesn't have angry [sic] about them'.

So, for some young people, it wouldn't be helpful to talk about their emotions with just anyone; the counsellor's particular qualities are what they find helpful. This links to the core attitudes of a counsellor who works within the person-centred approach that I described in Chapter 2. The counsellor's listening, understanding and accepting are what these young people found helpful.

What is happening in this process is a relational exchange where young people talk about their emotions and experience the CORE CONDITIONS from the counsellor. That seemed to lead to a cycle of self-esteem, self-efficacy, confidence and agency. In other words, through the relationship with the counsellor, young people felt better about themselves, better able to do the things they wanted to do, more confident generally and empowered as agents in their own lives.

The specifics of this cycle were different for each young person. For example, Stuart was spurred on by his experience of counselling to reassess his friendships: 'It kind of increased my self-esteem really, and I realised I'm not as bad as I think I am – before this thing I had friends, but they did stuff like talk behind my back – now I've got proper friends – because negative attitude was something that kept me back from making good friends.' After feeling valued in his relationship with the counsellor, Stuart came to expect more from his relationships with friends, and began to feel that he deserved to be treated with respect.

This process of increasing self-worth had many positive effects on the young people's lives, but a common theme was an improvement in relationships. For some, it gave them more confidence to socialise. Beth (age 13) talked about 'my confidence – like I feel much better and not as nervous as I was before – I'm starting to sit with my pals at lunchtime'. Before having counselling, she had told me that she felt too shy to talk to people at school and often ate lunch on her own for this reason. Kimberley (age 13) described how feeling valued and respected by the counsellor made her feel more assertive and better able to communicate with her family: 'I feel way different, I feel noticed now – it's because I've been able to talk to my Mum and Dad – I think I have more fun with them, I've got the courage to ask if we're allowed to play this game or that game.' Having had a positive experience of opening up in counselling meant Kimberley felt able to open up to her parents, which improved her relationship with them.

The process of increasing self-worth also had a positive impact on some of the young people's school work. Often this related to a greater feeling of self-efficacy and agency, as it did for Paul (age 15): 'I can work better in school when I try.' In other words, young people felt more confident in their ability to work at school, and took more responsibility for trying to achieve academically. Sometimes improvements in school work related directly to self-esteem, as for Stuart (age 16): 'I used to have thoughts like "I'm just going to end up failing this"… [counselling] made me work harder and try and achieve more, and try and not be, you know, a failure that I thought I was at the start.' This shows how demotivating low self-esteem can be, how it can impact on a young person's life in all sorts of ways, and how counselling can improve that.

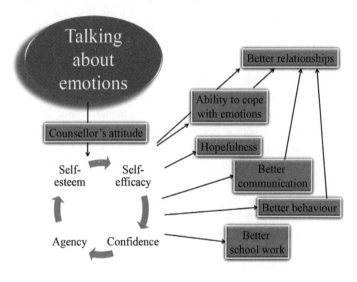

INSIGHT

The process of increasing self-worth tended to overlap with another process that related to developing insight. For some young people, talking about their emotions led them to reflect in a way that they may not have done before. Sometimes this came about simply through the young person talking about their emotions, but often it was linked to specific activities suggested by the counsellor. For instance, Rachel (age 14) described an activity suggested by her counsellor that helped her to understand her relationship with her dad better: 'I never even thought of my Dad until I started talking to [counsellor]… we use little pebbles and we make a family and make up a story about them… I made one for my Dad, and we went from there.' The activity seemed to help Rachel to reflect on her relationship with her dad in a way that she hadn't before, and so provided a framework for her to explore her feelings about family. Describing a similar activity, Kimberley said: 'When I'd finished I realised everyone was quite close… eventually it just all came to one corner because I was there, and it was like they were all dead special to me. I didn't actually realise that until I done it, so that helped me.' Kimberley's experience shows how a simple activity like using pebbles to map out significant relationships in a young person's life can make abstract ideas clearer for him or her.

Reflecting on feelings and other experiences through talking to a counsellor tended to lead to greater self-awareness as well as more understanding of others, and this in turn fed into the cycle of improved self-esteem, self-efficacy, confidence and agency that I mentioned before. Young people tended to move towards feeling more positive not only about themselves but also about other people, which again led to improvements in relationships. For example, Stuart reported a more positive view of the people around him, with reference to his family – '[Counselling] kind of got me trusting my parents more and being able to talk to them more about stuff like problems that are going on;' his friends – 'It's like seeing my friends actually supporting me if I ever need anything;' the teachers at school – 'The teachers are starting to believe in me properly,' and people in general: 'People are different, they're more kind hearted.'

For some of the young people, it seems that developing insight led to increased EMPATHY. Chloe described this process: 'I think on the whole [counselling] was a really good experience to have because it broadened my horizons. You think more about, like, who you are. Since I started I'm starting to properly understand and not think about just me – think about like, other people. I don't know, it's quite a big thing.' For both Chloe and Stuart, who were 16 at the time of counselling and therefore older than most of the clients mentioned here, counselling seems to have supported a natural part of their growing up and becoming more reflective about themselves and the people around them.

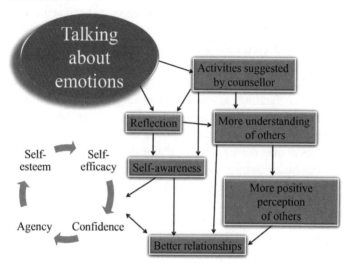

COPING STRATEGIES

Some young people reported that they had learned coping strategies from the counsellor, and found that they were better able to handle their emotions as a result. This process was most evident for the young men, and specifically related to coping with anger, which is a common reason for male pupils to start school-based counselling (Cooper, 2013). The counsellor offered particular coping mechanisms or relaxation techniques, which the young people were able to use in moments when anger might have overwhelmed them, and so feel more in control of their reactions. (See Chapter 2 of this book for examples of the various methods that school counsellors may use.) Paul (age 15) said: 'I've been able to cope with my anger a bit better – [Counsellor] says if I feel it go from green, amber to red, then amber is when you know you're about to… it's helped because I know when to calm down in a situation – I can feel it.' This is a simple technique to encourage young people to practise being more aware of their changing moods and choose to react differently to them.

Having more control over their emotions, most often anger, led to better behaviour and better relationships for these young people. Interestingly, in this process the counsellor's willingness to be relatively DIRECTIVE was important. Introducing a relaxation technique or suggesting a coping strategy for managing emotions may be considered outside a stance of non-directivity, and not all PERSON-CENTRED counsellors would be willing to work in this way.

Josh spoke about being able to handle angry outbursts by taking the counsellor's advice: 'I got somebody to talk to and, I don't know, she told me what to do if something went wrong.' It may be that the counsellor would not describe the interaction as telling Josh what to do, but from his perspective this was what he found helpful. In previous research on school-based counselling, young people have reported that advice and specific techniques are helpful, and although young people generally report positive views of school-based counselling, their criticisms tend to focus on a wish for a more active, DIRECTIVE approach (eg. Bondi et al, 2006; Lynass et al, 2012). It seems that school counsellors tend to be more reluctant than young people to work in a directive way.

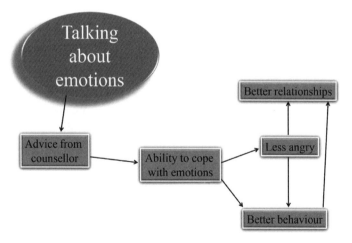

RELATIONAL SKILLS

Some of the young people seemed to use the experience of talking openly about their emotions with a counsellor as a way of practising and developing their relational skills. This in turn led to their having more open relationships with others, both in terms of talking and listening. Having the opportunity to practise these skills with the counsellor seemed to help them to communicate more effectively with other people in their lives. Young people often reported that their ability to talk openly with the counsellor improved as the counselling went on.

For instance, Beth said: 'When I first had [counselling], I was slightly nervous, but I've got a bit better at it.' Kimberley talked about the change in her listening skills: 'It's made me listen more, because what [counsellor] was saying, obviously I was listening to that, so it's like helped me learn to listen more.' She also described an instance where she was able to comfort someone else, attributing this to her experience of being listened to in counselling: 'She looked quite sad, so I was cheering her up. That was what [talking in counselling] done.' The overall sense is of young people developing relational skills through practising them regularly with the counsellor during sessions.

This process also suggests that young people are more likely to treat others with respect and caring after the experience of feeling respected and cared for by a counsellor. So perhaps the counsellor models a type of positive behaviour that young people are then likely to emulate in their relationships with other people. As in the other change processes mentioned, developing these relational skills led to improvements in other areas of young people's lives. Unsurprisingly, relationships generally improved when young people were more open and more receptive in their conversations. For some of the young people, listening and communicating more effectively improved their school work too. This could be because better relationships with teachers created a better environment for learning, as well as because strong communication skills are an important part of many academic subjects. Beth said: 'I'm sort of getting to really understand my teachers, I know what the teacher's talking about,' and Paul described how counselling had helped him with the presentation element of his English class: 'Last year I got a note for my talk because it was hard to do in front of the class because of my confidence... Talking to [counsellor], my confidence, it's helped me – I was scared to talk to anyone, so it's boosted my confidence a lot.' This demonstrates how counselling can help young people to feel more comfortable with speaking generally, which extends to public speaking – a key life skill.

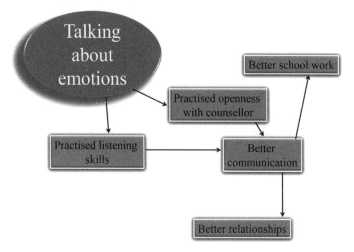

NEGATIVE PROCESSES

In these same interviews, the young people were asked about any negative changes they had experienced, and anything that was unhelpful about counselling. Although a small number of negative changes were mentioned, none of them were linked to unhelpful aspects of counselling. However, it was possible to draw some connections between unhelpful aspects of counselling and a relative lack of positive change. Based on this, two issues were identified that could have impeded change for some of the young clients.

The first issue was a difficulty with talking about emotions. This was a commonly reported unhelpful aspect of counselling for young people, who said that they often felt very nervous about opening up to the counsellor. The majority of the young people quickly overcame any discomfort about talking and it did not interfere with their positive change processes. But for others, the discomfort remained and presumably was not recognised or adequately addressed by the counsellor. It may be that the counsellors underestimated how nervous young people were about talking, or perhaps their responses to a young client's nerves did not succeed in putting them at ease. In the interviews the young people tended to relate this issue to wanting more active input from the counsellor, which has come up in research on school-based counselling before (Cooper, 2009). For instance Hannah said: 'Instead of just sitting talking, maybe more activities... just rather than sitting talking and not doing anything, sometimes it's just hard.'

It seems that the counsellor's non-directivity added to Hannah's discomfort and made it more difficult for her to be there. This suggests that incorporating some counsellor-led activities can serve a relational purpose by making young people feel more at ease in the counselling relationship. Activities, as well as being beneficial in themselves for some clients, might reduce anxiety for clients who do not want to direct their own process in counselling. Although the principle of non-directivity is empowering, it seems that some directivity from the counsellor can help to balance the power dynamic between them, as an adult, and the young client.

The second issue that seemed to impede positive change for some of the young people was the time limit on the counselling. The young people interviewed in this study were each offered one school term of weekly counselling sessions, which in practice amounted to about nine sessions. This was enough for most of them, but two found the time limit unhelpful. Not having enough sessions may be linked to difficulty talking about emotions in that some young people may need a longer time to become used to talking openly with a counsellor, and the counselling may come to an end before they have been able to experience significant benefits. They may use the whole period of counselling getting used to the process, which leaves no time for therapeutic work. This was the case for Rachel: 'When I first started [counselling], I didn't talk... After the first two [sessions] or something, I started talking.' Naturally, different people adjust to counselling differently, and this finding is a reminder that, while one school term of counselling may be sufficient for the majority of young people, some may need and/or want a longer period of counselling.

7

GOALS AND OUTCOMES IN SCHOOL-BASED COUNSELLING

As discussed in the last chapter, different young people achieve different outcomes from school-based counselling through different processes of change. OUTCOME MEASURES can help researchers to determine whether young people experience particular pre-defined changes, such as a reduction in psychological distress. But what do young people themselves want to change through school-based counselling? What kind of problems bring them to school-based counselling in the first place? Does school-based counselling mostly address school-related problems? Assuming that school-based counselling does go well, what are the outcomes for individual young people?

This chapter describes some of the outcome measures that are commonly used to evaluate school-based counselling, and counselling in general, with children and young people. Below are brief descriptions of three commonly used outcome measures to give some context to my points about goals and outcomes in school-based counselling. I have written in more detail about measures and more general issues around evaluation methods in a chapter in the *Handbook of Counselling Children and Young People* (McArthur & Cooper, 2015).

YP-CORE

The Young Person's Clinical Outcomes in Routine Evaluation outcome measure (usually referred to as the YP-CORE) is the most commonly used evaluation tool in school-based counselling in the UK. Its development is described in a paper by Twigg et al (2015). You can also find out more at www.coreims.co.uk. The YP-CORE is designed for young people aged 11–16 and therefore is not suitable for use in primary schools. It is an easy-to-use questionnaire designed for secondary school-age children and young people, with 10 statements and tick boxes for the client to show how often each statement has been true for them over the last week. For instance, for statements including 'It's been hard to go to sleep or stay asleep' (item 8) and 'I've felt unhappy' (item 9), the young client chooses from five possible responses: not at all, only occasionally, sometimes, often, most or all of the time. Because this measure looks at how someone has been feeling over the previous week, it can be used at the beginning of every counselling session and is so short that it doesn't take up a lot of time. It aims to measure psychological distress, and when I mention in this chapter research that has shown a reduction in psychological distress, this usually means a reduction in a young person's score on the YP-CORE.

Strengths and Difficulties Questionnaire

Another commonly used tool for evaluating counselling with children and young people, and in schools specifically, is the Strengths and Difficulties Questionnaire, or SDQ. This is the most widely used evaluation tool in Child and Adolescent Mental Health Services (CAMHS). It is described in more detail in a paper by Goodman and Goodman (2009), and you can download different versions of the measure at www.sdqinfo.com. There is a self-report version that is designed to be completed by young people aged 11–17. For younger children aged 3–4 and 4–16, there are versions that parents (parent-rated) and teachers (teacher-rated) can complete *about* the child. SDQ asks about the previous six months, so it is not appropriate for use at every session. It is made up of one subscale relating to pro-social behaviour (SDQ-PS) and four subscales relating to different kinds of distress: hyperactivity (SDQ-HA), peer problems (SDQ-PP), emotional symptoms (SDQ-ES) and conduct problems (SDQ-CP). The questionnaire is longer than the YP-CORE, at 25 items, and each item has three possible responses: not true, somewhat true and certainly true. The items include 'I am helpful if someone is hurt, upset or feeling ill' (item 9, part of SDQ-PS), and 'Other children or young people pick on me or bully me' (item 19, part of SDQ-PP).

Goal-Based Outcomes measure

Recently, the CAMHS Outcome and Research Consortium (CORC) developed a tool to measure young people's goals for counselling. Unlike the YP-CORE and the SDQ, the Goal-Based Outcomes (GBO) measure does not have a list of items that are rated by the young client. Instead, the young client and the counsellor (or sometimes a researcher) develop the items together, based on what the young client wants to get out of counselling. It is designed for young people of secondary school age (11–16), but it can be completed by an adult on behalf of younger children. It is described in more detail by Law and Jacob (2015) and can be downloaded from www.corc. uk.net. There is space on the questionnaire for young clients to record up to three personal goals for counselling, and they are asked to rate each of these goals according to how close they feel to achieving them, from 0 (goal not at all met) up to 10 (goal reached). Setting goals is a collaborative process between the client and the counsellor, and the goals are developed at the beginning of counselling and reviewed throughout.

What do young people want to change through school-based counselling?

We know from school-based counsellors' reports of 'presenting problems' what brings young people to counselling in the first place. Cooper (2013) has summarised research on presenting problems from three papers: Hill and colleagues (2011), McKenzie and colleagues (2011) and Cooper (2009). Table 1 shows the most common presenting problems according to counsellors' reports and roughly how prevalent each of these presenting problems are. The most common presenting problem is family issues, followed by anger, which affects more young men than young women. Other commonly reported presenting problems include behaviour, bereavement, bullying, self-worth, and relationship problems.

Table 1

Presenting problems as reported by counsellors	Prevalence
Family issues	About 33.3% of young clients
Anger	About 16% of young clients (About 25% of young male clients)
Behaviour	About 12% of young clients
Bereavement	About 10% of young clients
Bullying	About 10% of young clients
Self-worth	About 10% of young clients
Relationships	About 10% of young clients

These data come from counsellors' reports of young people's problems when they first come for school-based counselling. More recently, the Goal-Based Outcomes tool has given us data showing what young people themselves want to change through counselling. A recent study by Rupani and colleagues (2014) analysed data collected using the Goal-Based Outcomes tool in two RANDOMISED CONTROLLED TRIALS (RCTs) of school-based counselling (McArthur, Cooper & Berdondini, 2013; Pybis et al, 2015). The analysis revealed that the goals identified by young people are broadly similar to those identified by adults entering counselling. Interestingly, the young clients' goals did not fully correspond to previous research on counsellors' reports of presenting problems. The most commonly identified goal for young people was about increasing their self-confidence and self-acceptance (either generally or in relation to specific aspects of their life, such as their appearance). This was more often reported by young women. The second most commonly identified goal was to control or reduce anger, and this was more often reported by young men. Third were goals related to improving relationships with family members, which were again more commonly identified by young women. Often this involved improving communication or behaviour when with family, or coping with a change in family dynamics. The fourth most common category of goals related to either increasing happiness or decreasing feelings of distress, and the fifth was reducing anxiety or worry and increasing calmness, either in general or in relation to a specific aspect of the young person's life.

This research suggests a tendency for school counsellors to underestimate the extent that young people are troubled by self-esteem issues, anger and anxiety, and to overestimate the importance of family and relationship issues. Similarly, young people tend to phrase their goals in terms of changing how they feel, while counsellors are more likely to see their young clients' problems as contextual. It may be that this difference in perception is natural and reflects the counsellor's understanding of the bigger picture of a young person's life and perhaps the underlying causes of self-esteem issues, anger and anxiety. The difference doesn't necessarily indicate a lack of attunement between counsellor and client. However, we know that counselling is more likely to achieve better outcomes if the counsellor and the client agree about the therapeutic goals (Tryon & Winograd, 2002). So it is likely to be helpful if the counsellor and client discuss the therapeutic goals at the outset and revisit them throughout the counselling, to make sure they are in agreement.

WHAT CHANGES THROUGH SCHOOL-BASED COUNSELLING?

So far, no evidence has emerged that links levels of improvement in school-based counselling with particular presenting problems or particular goals (Cooper, 2013). In other words, research has not shown that some types of goal are *more likely* to be achieved through school-based counselling than others. But, overall, achievement of children and young people's personal goals is one of the biggest areas of change that research shows comes from school-based counselling, along with reduction in psychological distress. In other words, reducing distress and enabling young people to achieve their goals seem to be what school-based counselling does best. This suggests that young people who have counselling at school not only feel better *generally*; they also achieve the goals that are specific to their individual wants and needs.

If we look to QUALITATIVE research, we find a wide range of potential outcomes can result from school-based counselling. Young people's self-reported changes include finding it easier to talk about their feelings, being seen differently by others, improvements in school, more confidence/increased self-esteem, changes in thinking, and better behaviour, such as feeling more able to walk away from situations that make them angry (Lynass, Pyhktina & Cooper, 2012).

These outcomes broadly correspond to the experiences of the 14 young people I interviewed about their experience of school-based counselling (see chapter 6). The positive changes they described can be grouped into four broad categories: relationships, emotions, self and functioning. Positive changes in relationships included relationships with peers, family, teachers, and generally improved relational skills and attitudes to others. For instance, Neil (age 14) said, 'I feel I've got more friends' and 'I couldn't talk to anyone [before counselling]'. Emotional changes included feeling happier, less anxious, less angry and more able to cope with emotions. Some of the young people talked about an increased ability to cope with emotions generally; with others it related specifically to anxiety and/or anger. Michael (age 13) said, 'I've calmed down a wee bit'. Changes related to self included improvements in self-awareness, agency, self-esteem, confidence, hopefulness and self-efficacy. Changes related to aspects of functioning were improved school work, general focus or concentration, behaviour and sleep.

In the same way that school-based counselling can offer multiple pathways to change, different positive changes can overlap with and reinforce each other. For instance, feeling happier generally is likely to lead to young people feeling more positive about other aspects of their lives. Similarly, increased self-esteem could naturally lead to a young person feeling happier, as well as improvements in their relationships and functioning.

SCHOOL-RELATED PROBLEMS

The majority of young people say that they would rather access a counselling service in the school than go to a counselling service outside the school (Cooper, 2006; Quinn & Chan, 2009). However, we know from the research that the problems with which young people present, their goals and the positive changes they experience are not just school-related issues. This reinforces the argument for a national counselling service that is based in schools but independent from the school culture, unlike (say) in the US, where school-based counselling tends to have direct educational and vocational aims. At the same time, school-related issues do of course come up in school-based counselling, and the improvements we know it achieves in self-esteem and confidence are likely to help with school-specific issues such as being bullied at school.

In the case of bullying, changes self-reported by young people in school-based counselling research include feeling more able to stand up to bullies (Lynass, Pyhktina & Cooper, 2012; Cooper, 2004). One study also found that young people who began school-based counselling with problems relating to being bullied showed a more rapid decrease in their scores for peer problems (one of the subscales of the SDQ), suggesting that school-based counselling has a particular positive impact on relationships with peers for young people who are being bullied (McElearney et al, 2013). This is encouraging evidence that school-based counselling may contribute to empowering the victims of bullying.

Similarly, although counsellors in UK schools do not set out to address educational attainment or focus on it, school-based counselling seems to improve attainment indirectly. Benefits for school work seem to come up when young people are asked open questions about the changes they experience through school-based counselling, and two UK studies have looked specifically at the potential impact of school-based counselling on educational attainment and found positive results (Cooper et al, 2006; Rupani, Haughey & Cooper, 2012). The picture that emerges from this research, and from my own analysis of young people's change processes in school-based counselling described in the last chapter, is that improvements in school work come about indirectly when certain barriers to learning are removed. Feeling distressed seems to have the greatest negative effect on young people's *concentration* at school, presumably because their minds are preoccupied with whatever is distressing them. Being distressed also has a negative effect on a young person's motivation to attend school, their actual attendance, their motivation to study and to learn, and their relationships with teachers. So, if school-based counselling can reduce a young person's distress, it is easy to see how this could lead to other changes at school that then lead to better attainment. As well as positive changes in these areas, the accumulating evidence suggests that school-based counselling also increases a young person's participation in class and their confidence in relation to their school work.

8

EVIDENCE FOR THE EFFECTIVENESS
OF SCHOOL-BASED COUNSELLING

As a school counsellor who has spent years researching and writing about school-based counselling in UK secondary schools, obviously I believe that it benefits young people considerably. But how do we *know* that school-based counselling helps young people enough to justify its place in schools? To justify the future provision of counselling in schools, we have to be able to provide evidence that it really improves young people's lives and their life chances.

SCHOOL-BASED COUNSELLING RESEARCH

I have referenced various pieces of research on school-based counselling so far in this book. There are numerous evaluation studies that use formal measures like those I described in the previous chapter to evaluate how much change happens during school-based counselling. Cooper (2009) published a meta-analysis of 30 UK studies of school-based counselling that showed a large effect in reducing psychological distress. In statistics, EFFECT SIZES are a way of standardising results from different studies that may use different measures, so that they can be meaningfully compared with each other. EFFECT SIZES can be small, medium or large; the size describes the amount of change that comes about during a particular INTERVENTION. So, a large effect size for school-based counselling suggests that a large amount of positive change occurs for young people while they are having counselling at school. Cooper's findings have been supported by subsequent evaluation studies that have similarly demonstrated an association between school-based counselling and reductions in psychological distress (eg. Hill et al, 2011).

However, a key problem with most data on school-based counselling is that, if measures are taken only before and after counselling, young people who drop out of counselling before it reaches a natural end are not included in the analysis. So these data only tell part of the story. It stands to reason that young people who have a less positive experience of counselling may be more likely to end it prematurely. So results taken from only those young people who complete counselling may be positively skewed in favour of counselling. There may also be a PLACEBO EFFECT: simply taking part in a research study may be a more powerful factor in reducing young people's distress than counselling itself.

The placebo effect has long been recognised in medical research – the fact that even when participants are given pills with no active ingredient during a research trial, their medical condition tends to improve. It is possible that the hope that they will feel better has a positive impact in itself. Whatever the explanation, it seems likely that something similar happens in counselling research. Taking part in a study may include completing questionnaires about your feelings and having an assessment interview with a researcher, both of which could be experienced as helpful by young people in distress.

For all these reasons, these kinds of data cannot tell us for sure how much of the improvement they record is related to having school-based counselling. It may also simply be that young people will feel better over time anyway, regardless of whether they have counselling at school or not. In other words, feeling better could happen naturally and not actually as a result of counselling.

Research studies can be designed to address these limitations to some extent, but the issue of research methods in counselling is politically charged. There are conflicting views on how this kind of research should be conducted, and what constitutes evidence of effectiveness, as I explain below.

A HIERARCHY OF EVIDENCE

RANDOMISED CONTROLLED TRIALS (RCTs) carry the most weight politically in health research, because clinical guidelines groups (such as the National Institute for Health and Care Excellence

(NICE), and the Scottish Intercollegiate Guidelines Network (SIGN)) primarily base their recommendations on evidence from RCTs. Within the hierarchy of research evidence, RCT evidence is seen as the 'gold standard'. In fact, RCTs are seen by many as necessary to establish whether an INTERVENTION, like counselling, is effective. However others see RCTs as an inappropriate method of researching a human interaction like counselling.

An RCT works by randomly assigning participants into two or more groups that can then be compared against each other. The basic principle is to compare a group of people who have had a particular intervention with a group who have not. So, you would measure for both groups something that you think might change as a result of the intervention and then, after a specified amount of time, measure both groups again and compare the results. RCTs were originally designed to test medical interventions, and using a medical example is the easiest way to explain how they work. For instance, to test a drug that researchers believe has the potential to lower blood pressure, you could measure the blood pressure of each participant, then randomly assign participants to one of two groups. Only one of the groups will receive the drug treatment; the other will not and will act as a 'control'. Sometimes, the participants know whether or not they are receiving the treatment; in other trials they won't – they'll be given a PLACEBO pill. This is called a 'blind' trial.

However, this 'blind' option is only possible with medication. For most other types of intervention, including counselling, participants will obviously know whether or not they have received the intervention. It may be that the control group receives no intervention, or the control group might receive a comparable treatment instead. So, if the intervention group has counselling, the control group could either have no input at all, or something like a self-help programme. In more complex RCTs there can also be more than one control condition or alternative treatment. So, in the same RCT you could have one group having counselling, one group taking part in a self-help programme, and a third group having no input at all.

Random allocation is used because it should ensure that the influence of any individual differences between the participants is evened out and any differences that emerge will be due to the INTERVENTIONS and not anything else, like chance. The larger the number of participants in an RCT, the more powerful the results are, because larger numbers in each group mean that the individual differences between them are even less likely to influence the results. The researchers decide on a specific period of time for the intervention, and measures are taken from both groups before and after that period of time. So, for counselling children and young people, the measures I referenced in the previous chapter might be used to look at differences between those who have had counselling and those who have not.

As a research method, RCTs are traditionally not popular among counsellors, and the assumptions underlying an RCT do not fit well with the values of a humanistic approach. As I mentioned, RCTs were designed to assess medical interventions like drugs, and to view counselling as a 'treatment' overlooks its essence as a unique relationship between two human beings. Clients respond in unique and unpredictable ways to the therapeutic relationship they form with the counsellor, who is also a unique human being. Critics argue that RCTs treat human distress as a technical problem to be fixed, whereas how people feel and why is far more complex, and is dependent on a huge number of factors. The wisdom of bowing to political demand by conducting RCTs of humanistic counselling has been questioned, as have the ethics of involving young people in what could be experienced as a dehumanising process (eg. Rogers, Maidman & House, 2011). On the other hand, Cooper (2011) has argued the case for humanistic counsellors to engage in RCT research, and I have supported these arguments with my own account of attempting to use an RCT method within a broadly humanistic approach (McArthur, 2011).

Despite its dominance and its continuing reputation as the 'gold standard', RCT evidence is undoubtedly limited in its capacity to assess the full value of counselling. QUALITATIVE research can provide a richer understanding of the real life impact of school-based counselling on young people. However, in the current political and academic climate, demonstrating the effectiveness of counselling with RCT evidence is essential for its continued provision, and we hope its expansion, in schools.

EFFECTIVENESS RESEARCH

To date, a small number of researchers (including me) have conducted RCTs of school-based counselling in three small-scale pilot studies (Cooper et al, 2010; McArthur et al, 2013; Pybis et al, 2015). Each of these studies compares young people receiving school-based counselling with others on a waiting list for counselling over an equivalent period of time (six weeks in the first study and 10–12 weeks in the other two). In all the studies all participants had counselling at some point, but those who were randomly allocated to the control group had to wait before beginning counselling. The studies were designed in this way so that all the young people involved had the opportunity to have counselling, but the researchers still had the opportunity (at the end of the waiting period) to compare those who had already attended counselling with those who had not.

Taken together, these three studies have a total sample of 90 young people, and their collective results demonstrate that school-based counselling leads to significantly lower distress and greater progress towards achieving personal goals (Cooper, 2013). These results are encouraging, suggesting that the positive effects of school-based counselling shown in previous research stand up to the more rigorous RCT method. The positive results are comparable with changes that research shows come about from most forms of adult and child psychotherapy (Kazdin, 2004; Lambert & Ogles, 2004; Weisz et al, 1995). This research paves the way for larger, more powerful studies testing the effectiveness of humanistic counselling.

In addition to RCTs, developments in practice-based research continue to add to the evidence base for school-based counselling. For instance, a study by Cooper and colleagues

(2014) evaluated a school-based counselling service by using weekly session-by-session OUTCOME MEASURES (in this case, clients completed the YP-CORE at every counselling session). This overcomes the problem of losing data from young people who drop out of counselling before it reaches a natural end, so it is more reliable than previous studies. This study found a large positive effect for school-based counselling in terms of reducing psychological distress – in fact larger than in previous research on school-based counselling (Cooper, 2009). So, as well as supporting the effectiveness of school-based counselling for reducing distress, this study adds to a growing body of evidence that completing evaluation measures as part of counselling can be beneficial for clients.

Another study of primary school-based counselling used systematic feedback with young children (Cooper et al, 2012). This means that the measures were used actively with the young clients within the counselling sessions so that they could see their own progress. This study found that the systematic feedback seemed to double the positive impact of counselling on psychological distress. So, not only is there growing evidence that having counselling at school is beneficial for clients; there are also clear indications that participating in research studies is helpful in itself. In addition, the evaluation process seems to be a positive experience for clients and counsellors alike (Hanley, Sefi & Lennie, 2011; Cooper et al, 2010). In other words, taking part in research is not only associated with improving therapeutic outcomes; clients and counsellors also seem to enjoy the experience.

PRACTICE RESEARCH NETWORKS (PRNs)

Despite this, there is some evidence that many counsellors, in both child and adult services, are reluctant to participate in research (Daniel & McLeod, 2006). This is especially the case for those who identify with a humanistic approach. However, counselling practitioners are now widely encouraged to engage in research activity, and those in training are expected to understand and participate in this kind of work (Dunnett, Cooper & Wheeler, 2007; Wheeler & Elliott, 2008).

The BACP has launched a practice research network specifically dedicated to counselling with children and young people (CYP PRN). It aims to promote the inter-relationship of research and practice and create a sustainable network of practitioner-researchers to engage in ethical practice-based research in order to secure the future of counselling as a profession. PRNs generally are intended to close the gap between practitioners and researchers, empowering and informing both and leading to collaborative, high quality evidence. In order to address the question of how effective counselling really is, a range of different perspectives, tools and methods are required, balancing scientific rigour with clinical relevance. It would be in keeping with good research practice if QUALITATIVE and QUANTITATIVE research were both harnessed in this endeavour.

THE FUTURE OF SCHOOL-BASED COUNSELLING

The body of evidence now developing for school-based counselling as an effective response to psychological distress in young people suggests that widening access to counselling services in UK schools is appropriate and desirable. In early 2016 a large-scale RCT of school-based counselling across 18 secondary schools was launched with funding from the Economic and Social Research Council, and led by the University of Roehampton. In addition, both the Children's Commissioner for England and the Department for Education's mental health champion have recently called for all schools to provide a counselling service for pupils.

Personally, I hope that access to school-based counselling will increase until it is available to every child and young person. I believe that this will have a life-long benefit for all young people across the UK. I also hope that establishing this kind of service as standard in schools will have a much wider impact on social attitudes to mental distress, wellbeing and emotional support. In addition, I hope that the practice of school-based counselling will continue to evolve and improve to meet the various needs of young people in their diversity. Some ideas for improving practice that I have already discussed in this book include the use of session-by-session outcome measures, willingness to incorporate a wider breadth of techniques and approaches (especially in cases where young people have difficulty opening up) and more flexibility around the duration of counselling. Greater understanding of diversity in race, culture and gender is also needed in today's multi-dimensional world. And, of course, more research is also important for the profession to inform understanding of the client group and their needs in order to continually improve counselling practice.

FURTHER RESOURCES

Children and Young People Practice Research Network
www.bacp.co.uk/schools
A practice research network established by the British Association for Counselling and Psychotherapy (BACP) that aims to encourage collaboration between researchers and counsellors working with children and young people (in schools and elsewhere) across the UK. It is free to join, and members are able to download a toolkit for collecting outcome measures.

CAMHS Outcomes Research Consortium (CORC)
www.chimat.org.uk/resource/item.aspx?RID=84535
A collaboration between child and adolescent mental health services (CAMHS) across the UK with the aim of instituting a common model of routine outcome evaluation and analysis of the data collected. The website provides access to a range of relevant information resources.

Triangle
www.triangle.org.uk
A Brighton-based training and consultancy organisation that specialises in advanced communication skills with very young children and working with children and young people who have communication impairments.

Young Minds
www.youngminds.org.uk
A UK-wide charity that campaigns to raise awareness and improve emotional wellbeing and mental health for children and young people.

Place2Be
www.place2be.org.uk
A UK-wide charity providing counselling services in primary
and secondary schools.

Youth Access
www.youthaccess.org.uk
The national membership organisation for young people's
information, advice, counselling and support services (YIACS).
Youth Access provides the training, resources, research,
campaigning and other infrastructure support to ensure that
high quality services, modelled on evidence-based approaches,
exist to meet young people's needs.

JOURNALS

BACP Children and Young People
The quarterly journal for the BACP Children and Young People
division for counsellors working with these age groups
www.bacpcyp.org.uk

The British Journal of Guidance and Counselling
A specialist journal published five times a year by Routledge.
It published a special issue on counselling in schools in 2012
(Volume 40, Issue 5).
www.tandfonline.com/toc/cbjg20/40/5

Counselling & Psychotherapy Research
BACP's research journal, published quarterly in association with
John Wiley & Sons, with frequent papers on school counselling
issues.
http://onlinelibrary.wiley.com/journal/10.1002/(ISSN)1746-1405

Advances in School Mental Health Promotion
Published by Routledge for professionals with an interest
in promoting mental health in schools through international

dialogue, collaboration and action. ASMHP publishes empirical and scholarly work that emphasises the interconnected nature of research, policy, training and practice in the field of school mental health.

www.tandfonline.com/loi/rasm20#.VsyQN5yLShc

Therapy Today

The monthly (published 10 times a year) membership journal of BACP, with regular articles on children and young people's mental health and news and news features on specific, wider and related policy and professional issues.

www.therapytoday.net

WEBSITES

MindEd

www.minded.org.uk

A free, open access e-learning resource for professionals in a range of roles concerned with children and young people's mental health. The Counselling MindEd section was developed by BACP with funding from the Department of Health, with content written by leading trainers and practitioners in the field, and is intended to supplement face-to-face training for counsellors working with children and young people.

BACP

www.bacp.co.uk/research/publications/School_Counselling.php

The BACP website has a section specifically for research on school-based counselling where you can download free research reports relevant to school-based counselling and children and young people's emotional and mental wellbeing.

FURTHER READING

Escher S, Romme M (2012). *Young People Hearing Voices: what you need to know and what you can do* (2nd edition). Monmouth: PCCS Books.

Keys S, Walshaw T (2008). *Person-centred Work with Children and Young People: UK practitioner perspectives*. Ross-on-Wye: PCCS Books.

Lines D (2011). *Brief Counselling in Schools: working with young people from 11 to 18*. Sage: London.

Newnes C (2015). *Children in Society: politics, policies and interventions*. Monmouth: PCCS Books.

Pattison S, Robson M, Beynon A (2014). *The Handbook of Counselling Children and Young People*. London: Sage.

Stapert M, Verlieefde E (2008). *Focusing with Children: the art of communicating with children at school and at home*. Ross-on-Wye: PCCS Books.

Timimi S (2009). *A Straight Talking Introduction to Children's Mental Health Problems*. Monmouth: PCCS Books.

GLOSSARY

BEHAVIOURISM – A school of psychology founded in the 1920s by John Watson that focuses exclusively on inputs or stimuli from the outside world and the resulting behaviour. The internal conditions of the person are of no interest at all. Although it has an influence in many areas of psychology, many people find it does not represent their experience of the world and so reject it.

BOUNDARIES – Limits or borders between activities. For example, it is good practice to have a clear, single professional relationship with a client – a counsellor should not see their friends or relatives as clients. So there is a professional BOUNDARY between friendship and counselling.

COGNITIVE BEHAVIOUR THERAPY – A 'school' of counselling/ therapy based on theories that derive from cognitive theory – ie. prime importance is given to rational thought processes and behaviours that logically follow from them.

CONGRUENCE – Has many meanings in counselling, but most often means real or genuine – for example, not trying to appear to be an expert.

CORE CONDITIONS (also known as CONDITIONS OF WORTH) – Coined by Carl Rogers to mean the conditions of value placed on you by someone else – for example, 'If you want me to love you, you must sit still and be quiet and polite'.

CONTRACT – An agreement between the therapist and the client that determines the kind of helping relationship it will be. If it is to be a counselling relationship, the contract establishes issues like the level of confidentiality offered, number and length of sessions, complaints procedures etc. It also will cover any legal rights and responsibilities, such as those in the current version of the Children Act.

DIRECTIVE/NON-DIRECTIVE APPROACH – Developed by Carl Rogers in the 1950s. The therapist adopts a strictly non-expert stance towards the client; instead of giving advice, he or she listens to and facilitates the client's own internal wisdom.

EFFECT SIZE – The quantifiable size of the improvement felt by the client as a result of the therapy – how much the client has benefitted from the specific INTERVENTION. In research an overall effect size t is often calculated from a number of studies so that small, overly positive or negative results are averaged out.

EMPATHY – Trying to see the world from the other person's point of view, as if it were your own.

EXISTENTIAL [PHILOSOPHY] – Relates to the philosophy of human existence and our experience of living-in-the-world. There is a very wide variety of thought within this philosophical tradition, some of it contradicting other parts. To see how this relates to existential counselling, read Mick Cooper's *The Existential Counselling Primer* (2012), which helpfully summarises the many different types based on different strands of existential philosophy.

GESTALT THERAPY – Based loosely on the Gestalt school of psychology developed in the 1940s, 50s and 60s by Fritz Perls and his associates in the US. Gestalt is a German word meaning 'whole', so Gestalt therapy is a holistic therapy (human beings should be seen as whole organisms, mind and body as one), not a reductionist one (splitting the person into parts). Distress is caused by incomplete Gestalts, or 'wholes' in a person's life (ie. 'unfinished business').

HUMANISTIC PSYCHOLOGY – A reaction to mechanistic, reductionist BEHAVIOURISM and PSYCHOANALYSIS, with its notions of an uncontrollable, unknowable unconscious and inherent 'dark side'. Dubbed the 'third force' in psychology, and founded by, among others, Carl Rogers and Abraham Maslow, humanistic psychology emphasises the positivity and responsibility of human beings and their drive towards fulfilment and self-actualisation.

INTEGRATIVE COUNSELLING – Any approach that blends, or integrates, theory or practices (techniques) from other approaches. There are many types of integrative counselling, and in most cases each counsellor's version is unique to them.

INTERVENTION – Strictly speaking it means 'interference' (to stop something, to intervene). Often used to mean a response or action by a counsellor or other helping professional such as a social worker, probation officer etc. The term is not often used in humanistic counselling, but if used it still means the counsellor's response.

MANUALISING – The creation of step-by-step instructions (a manual) on how to conduct a particular therapy or INTERVENTION. Helpful in research to ensure that the therapeutic treatment being tested is delivered in exactly the same way.

MEDICAL MODEL (OF MENTAL 'ILLNESS') – The system used by psychiatrists and majority of mental health professionals in the Western world to understand and classify psychological distress. It is a medical classification system based on the similarity of symptoms or experiences, not on cause-and-effect relationships. It mimics a medical model of physical disease. Many counsellors think it is not a good fit for understanding psychological distress.

OUTCOME (MEASURES) – The measure of how a client feels at the end of therapy against an external yardstick, such as an anxiety, depression or 'adjustment' scale or other psychological test. It is not the same as a 'change status' measure, which measures improvement by comparing how the client feels now with how they felt when they started counselling.

PERSON-CENTRED COUNSELLING – Developed by Carl Rogers in the 1940s, based on the idea that, under the right conditions (non-judgmental listening without giving advice), the client will find their own solutions to their problems.

PLACEBO EFFECT – A placebo is a benign or non-active 'treatment' that simulates a medical or effective treatment. It is commonly used to describe a pill with no active ingredients, or a psychological intervention known to have no active effects that is passed off as a treatment. Any effect derived from such treatment is called a 'placebo effect'.

POSITIVE PSYCHOLOGY – A way of studying psychology that emphasises human potential rather than human deficiencies. Many ways of looking at psychology concentrate on assumed abnormalities or failings. Positive psychology concentrates on strengths that enable thriving.

PSYCHOANALYSIS/PSYCHOANALYTIC – A school of psychology originated by and based on the work of Sigmund Freud. The method involves the client talking about whatever they want while the therapist minimally directs and offers interpretation based on Freud's theories of the unconscious and how it affects conscious life.

PSYCHODYNAMIC COUNSELLING – Derived from the work of Freud and later psychoanalytic theorists (see above). It tries to help clients understand their unconscious processes (things they are not immediately aware of) that might be the cause of their distress. The method is more dynamic than psychoanalysis, with the counsellor more actively offering observations and insights.

QUALITATIVE (RESEARCH METHODS) – Research that is concerned with the *qualities* of experience and human behaviour, as opposed to the *quantities*.

QUANTITATIVE (RESEARCH METHODS) – Concerned with experience and human behaviour that can be counted, such as the number of episodes of depression someone experiences in a year, or panic attacks in a week.

RANDOMISED CONTROLLED TRIALS – A research method in which clients are allocated randomly (ie. using no particular system) to either a 'treatment' group (to receive the treatment under investigation) or a 'control' group (which receives either no treatment or some standard default 'treatment as usual'). The theory is that, if all other conditions are exactly the same, any differences in outcomes must be due to the differences between the treatments.

REFLEXIVE PRACTICE – Practising in a way that acknowledges the person of the counsellor as a key instrument in the change process. Reflexive means self-referent, or referring back to one's self.

SUPERVISION – All professional counsellors must have a supervisor with whom they meet regularly to discuss cases. Supervisors are experienced therapists who help the counsellor work with difficulties or particular situations that may arise with clients.

SELF-ACTUALISATION – This term is used differently in different theories, but most share an understanding of actualisation as 'becoming' or 'achieving potential'. So self-actualisation means becoming your self or true self, or achieving your full potential to be yourself.

UNCONDITIONAL POSITIVE REGARD – Being non-judgmental; regarding someone as a human being worthy of respect, regardless of their behaviour. This is important so that clients do not feel judged by the counsellor.

REFERENCES

Axline VM (1964). *Dibs in Search of Self*. Boston: Houghton-Mifflin.

British Association for Counselling and Psychotherapy (BACP) (2016). *Ethical Framework for the Counselling Professions*. Lutterworth: BACP.

Baginsky W (2004). *School Counselling in England, Wales and Northern Ireland: a review*. London: NSPCC. www.safespacetherapy.co.uk/ media/schoolcounselling_wdf48931.pdf (accessed 24 November, 2015).

Baskin TW, Slaten CD, Crosby NR, Pufahl T, Schneller CL, Ladell M (2010). Efficacy of counseling and psychotherapy in schools: a meta-analytic review of treatment outcome studies. *The Counseling Psychologist 38*: 878–903. doi:10.1177/0011000010369497.

Belfer ML (2008). Child and adolescent mental health disorders: the magnitude of the problem across the globe. *Journal of Child Psychology and Psychiatry 49*: 226–236.

Biddle L, Donovan J, Sharp D, Gunnell D (2007). Explaining non-help-seeking amongst young adults with mental distress: a dynamic interpretive model of illness behavior. *Sociology of Health & Illness 29*(7): 983–1002.

Bondi L, Forbat L, Gallagher M, Plows V, Prior S (2006). *Evaluation of the Youth Counselling Service*. Edinburgh: University of Edinburgh.

Brent DA, Perper JA, Moritz G, Allman C, Friend A, Roth C, Schweers J, Balach L, Baugher M (1993). Psychiatric risk factors for adolescent suicide: a case-control study. *Journal of the American Academy of Child & Adolescent Psychiatry 32*(3): 521–529.

Central Advisory Council for Education (England) (1963). *Half Our Future: a report of the Central Advisory Council for Education (England) (The Newsome Report)*. London: Her Majesty's Stationery Office. www.educationengland.org.uk/documents/newsom/ newsom1963.html (accessed 20 February 2016).

Charura D (2012). 'What's a disrupted and traumatic childhood got to do with it?' Exploring therapeutic ways of working following childhood disruption with asylum seekers' concept of self and identity in adulthood. Paper presented at 'Displaced Childhoods: Oral History and Traumatic Experiences', the Annual Conference of the UK Oral History Society, Solent University, Southampton, UK.

Children's Commissioner for Wales (2004). *Clywch Report on the Examination of the Children's Commissioner for Wales into Allegations of Child Sexual Abuse in a School Setting.* Swansea: Children's Commissioner for Wales. https://www.childcomwales. org.uk/uploads/publications/70.pdf (accessed 19 February, 2016).

Cooper M (2004). *Counselling in Schools Project: evaluation report.* Glasgow: University of Strathclyde.

Cooper M (2006). Scottish secondary school students' preferences for location, format of counselling and sex of counsellor. *School Psychology International 27*(5): 627–638.

Cooper M (2009). Counselling in UK secondary schools: a comprehensive review of audit and evaluation data. *Counselling and Psychotherapy Research 9*(3): 137–150.

Cooper M (2011). Meeting the demand for evidence-based practice. *Therapy Today 22*(4):10–16.

Cooper M (2012). *The Existential Counselling Primer.* Ross-on-Wye: PCCS Books.

Cooper M (2013). *School-Based Counselling in UK Secondary Schools: a review and critical evaluation.* Glasgow: University of Strathclyde.

Cooper M, Freire E, Cunningham L, Lidstone E, McGinnis S, Ogden N (2006). *Counselling in Schools Project Phase II: evaluation report.* Glasgow: Counselling Unit, University of Strathclyde. http:// strathprints.strath.ac.uk/26793/ (accessed 21 February 2016).

Cooper M, Freire E, McGinnis S, Carrick L (2014). School-based humanistic counselling for psychological distress in young people: a cohort study using a low attrition sample. *Counselling and Psychotherapy Research 14*(3): 165–246. doi 10.1080/14733145.2014.929415.

Cooper M, Rowland N, McArthur K, Pattison S, Cromarty K, Richards K (2010). Randomised controlled trial of school-based humanistic counselling for emotional distress in young people: feasibility study and preliminary indications of efficacy. *Child and Adolescent Psychiatry and Mental Health 4*(1): 1–12.

Cooper M, Stewart D, Sparks JA, Bunting L (2012). School-based counseling using systematic feedback: a cohort study evaluating outcomes and predictors of change. *Psychotherapy Research 23*(4): 474–488. doi: 10.1080/10503307.2012.735777.

Daniel T, McLeod J (2006). Weighing up the evidence: a qualitative analysis of how person-centred counsellors evaluate the effectiveness of their practice. *Counselling and Psychotherapy Research 6*(4): 244–249.

Department for Education (2016). *Counselling in Schools: a blueprint for the future*. London: Department for Education. www.gov.uk/government/uploads/system/uploads/attachment_data/file/497825/Counselling_in_schools.pdf (accessed 19 February 2016).

Department of Health/NHS England (2015). *Future in Mind: promoting and protecting and improving our children and young people's mental health and wellbeing*. London: Department of Health/NHS England. www.gov.uk/government/uploads/system/uploads/attachment_data/file/414024/Childrens_Mental_Health.pdf (accessed 19 February 2016).

Dhillon-Stevens H (2004). *Healing inside and outside: an examination of dialogic encounters in the area of anti-oppressive practice in counselling and psychotherapy*. PhD thesis. London: Middlesex University.

Dimmitt C, Carey J, Hatch T (2007). *Evidence-Based School Counseling: making a difference with data-driven practices*. Thousand Oaks, CA: Corwin Press.

Dunnett A, Cooper M, Wheeler S (2007). *A Core Curriculum for Counselling and Psychotherapy*. Lutterworth: BACP.

Ellis E, Cooper N (2013). Silenced: the Black student experience. *Therapy Today 24*(10): 14–19.

Fergusson DM, Horwood LJ, Beautrais AL (1999). Is sexual orientation related to mental health problems and suicidality in young people? *Archives of General Psychiatry 56*(10): 876–880.

Freeman H (2013). Check your privilege! Whatever that means. *The Guardian* 5 June.

Geller B, Zimerman B, Williams M, Bolhofner K, Craney JL (2001). Adult psychosocial outcome of prepubertal major depressive disorder. *Journal of the American Academy of Child and Adolescent Psychiatry 40*: 673–677.

Goodman A, Goodman R (2009). Strengths and difficulties questionnaire as a dimensional measure of child mental health. *Journal of the American Academy of Child and Adolescent Psychiatry 48*: 400–403.

Goodwin RD, Davidson KW, Keyes K (2009). Mental disorders and cardiovascular disease among adults in the United States. *Journal of Psychiatric Research 43*(3): 239–246.

Grossman AH, D'Augeli AR (2007). Transgender youth and life threatening behaviors. *Suicide and Life Threatening Behavior 37*(5): 527–537.

Guasp A (2012). *The School Report: the experiences of gay young people in Britain's schools in 2012*. London/Cambridge: Stonewall/ University of Cambridge Centre for Family Research. https://www. stonewall.org.uk/sites/default/files/The_School_Report__2012_. pdf (accessed 21 February 2016).

Hanley T, Barlow A, Humphrey N, Jenkins P, Wigelsworth M (2012). *A Scoping Review of the Access to Secondary School Counselling*. Manchester: School of Education, University of Manchester.

Hanley T, Sefi A, Lennie C (2011). Practice-based evidence in school-based counselling. *Counselling and Psychotherapy Research 11*(4): 300–309.

Harris B (2013). *International School-Based Counselling: scoping report*. Lutterworth: BACP/CounsellingMindEd.

Hill A, Roth A, Cooper M (2014). *The Competences Required to Deliver Effective Humanistic Counselling for Young People: counsellor's guide*. Lutterworth: BACP. www.bacp.co.uk/research/competences/ cyp_competences.php (accessed 28 March, 2016).

Hill A, Cooper M, Pybis J, Cromarty K, Pattison S, Spong S, Dowd C, Leahy C, Couchman A, Rogers J, Smith K, Maybanks N (2011). *Evaluation of the Welsh School-Based Counselling Strategy*. Cardiff: Welsh Government Social Research.

Jenkins P (2010). Child protection and the duty to refer. *BACP Children & Young People, March*: 17–20.

Jenkins P (2015). Law and policy. In: Pattison S, Robson M, Beynon A (eds). *The Handbook of Counselling Children and Young People*. London: Sage (pp259–276).

Jenkins P, Palmer J (2012). 'At risk of harm?' An exploratory survey of school counsellors in the UK, their perceptions of confidentiality, information sharing and risk management. *British Journal of Guidance and Counselling 40*(5): 545–599.

Jenkins P, Polat F (2006). The Children Act 2004 and implications for counselling in schools in England and Wales. *Pastoral Care in Education 24*(2): 7–14.

Johnstone L (2014). *A Straight Talking Introduction to Psychiatric Diagnosis*. Monmouth: PCCS Books.

Kazdin AE (2004). Psychotherapy for children and adolescents. In: Lambert MJ (ed). *Bergin and Garfield's Handbook of Psychotherapy and Behavior Change (5th ed)*. Chicago, IL: John Wiley & Sons (pp 543–589).

Kessler RC, Berglund P, Demler O, Jin R, Merikangas KR, Walters EE (2005). Lifetime prevalence and age-of-onset distributions of DSM-

IV disorders in the national comorbidity survey replication. *Archives of General Psychiatry 62*: 593–602.

Lago C (2007). Counselling across difference and diversity. In: Cooper M, O'Hara M, Schmidt PF, Wyatt G (eds). *The Handbook of Person-Centred Psychotherapy and Counselling*. Basingstoke: Palgrave Macmillan.

Lago C (2011). *The Handbook of Transcultural Counselling and Psychotherapy*. Maidenhead: Open University Press.

Lago C, Smith B (2010). *Anti-Discriminatory Practice in Counselling & Psychotherapy*. London: Sage.

Lambert MJ, Ogles BM (2004). The efficacy and effectiveness of psychotherapy. In: Lambert MJ (ed). *Bergin and Garfield's Handbook of Psychotherapy and Behavior Change (5th ed)*. Chicago: John Wiley & Sons (pp139–193).

Law D, Jacob J (2015). *Goals and Goal-Based Outcomes (GBOs): some useful information (3rd ed)*. London: CAMHS Press. https://www.ucl.ac.uk/ebpu/docs/publication_files/Goals_booklet_3rd_ed (accessed 20 February 2016).

Lines D (2010). The duty to refer. *BACP Children & Young People, June*: 30–31.

Livingstone S, Gorzig A (2014). When adolescents receive sexual messages on the internet: explaining experiences of risk and harm. *Computers in Human Behaviour 33*: 8–15.

Lynass R, Pyhktina O, Cooper M (2012). A thematic analysis of young people's experience of counselling in secondary schools in the UK. *Counselling and Psychotherapy Research 12*(1): 53–62.

McArthur K (2011). RCTs: a personal experience. *Therapy Today 22*(7): 24–25.

McArthur K, Cooper M (2015). Evaluating counselling. In: Pattison S, Robson M, Beynon A (eds). *The Handbook of Counselling Children and Young People*. London: Sage (pp244–256).

McArthur K, Cooper M, Berdondini L (2013). School-based humanistic counseling for psychological distress in young people: pilot randomized controlled trial. *Psychotherapy Research 23*(3): 355–365. doi:10.1080/10503307.2012.726750.

McArthur K, Cooper M, Berdondini L (2015). Change processes in school-based humanistic counselling. *Counselling and Psychotherapy Research*. doi: 10.1002/capr.12061

McElearney A, Adamson G, Shevlin M, Bunting B (2013). Impact evaluation of a school-based counselling intervention in Northern

Ireland: is it effective for pupils who have been bullied? *Child Care in Practice 19*(1): 4–22.

McGinnis S, Jenkins P (eds) (2009). *Good Practice Guidance for Counselling in Schools (4th ed)*. Lutterworth: BACP.

McKenzie K, Murray G, Prior S, Stark L (2011). An evaluation of a school counselling service with direct links to Child and Adolescent Mental Health (CAMH) Services. *British Journal of Guidance and Counselling 39*(1): 67–82.

Moncrieff J (2014). *A Straight Talking Introduction to Psychiatric Diagnosis*. Monmouth: PCCS Books.

Myers F, McCollam A, Woodhouse A (2005). *National Programme for Improving Mental Health and Well-being. Addressing Mental Health Inequalities in Scotland – Equal Mind*s. Edinburgh: Scottish Executive.

Murphy M, Fonagy P (2013). Mental health problems in children and young people. In: Davies SC. *Our Children Deserve Better: prevention pays. Annual Report of the Chief Medical Officer 2012*. London: Department of Health.

National Society for the Prevention of Cruelty to Children (2008). *Evidence to Lord Laming's Review of Child Protection*. London: NSPCC.

National Records of Scotland (2015). *Life Expectancy for Administrative Areas within Scotland 2012-2014*. Edinburgh: National Records of Scotland. www.nrscotland.gov.uk/statistics-and-data/statistics/statistics-by-theme/life-expectancy/life-expectancy-in-scottish-areas/2012-2014 (accessed 20 February 2016).

Pattison S, Charura D, McAndrew T (2015). Diversity. In: Pattison S, Robson M, Beynon A (eds). *The Handbook of Counselling Children and Young People*. London: Sage (pp 294–307).

Pybis J, Cooper M, Hill A, Cromarty K, Levesley R, Murdoch J, Turner N (2015). Pilot randomised controlled trial of school-based humanistic counselling for psychological distress in young people: outcomes and methodological reflections. *Counselling and Psychotherapy Research 15*(4): 241–250. doi: 10.1002/capr.12009

Quinn P, Chan S (2009). Secondary school students' preferences for location, format of counselling and gender of counsellor: a replication study based in Northern Ireland. *Counselling and Psychotherapy Research 9*(3): 204–209.

Raghavan R, Patel P (2005). *Learning Disabilities and Mental Health: a nursing perspective*. Oxford: Blackwell.

Rapley M, Moncrieff J, Dillon J (2011). *De-medicalizing misery:*

psychiatry, psychology and the human condition. Basingstoke: Palgrave Macmillan.

Read J (2004). Poverty, ethnicity and gender. In: Read J, Bentall R, Mosher L (eds). *Models of Madness: psychological, social and biological approaches to schizophrenia*. London: Brunner/ Routledge (pp161–194).

Rogers CR (1951). *Client-Centered Therapy: its current practice, implications and theory*. London: Constable.

Rogers CR (1957). The necessary and sufficient conditions of therapeutic personality change. *Journal of Consulting Psychology 21*: 95–103.

Rogers CR (1959). A theory of therapy, personality and interpersonal relationships as developed in the client-centered framework. In: Koch S (ed). *Psychology: a study of science, vol. 3*. New York: McGraw-Hill (pp184–256).

Rogers A, Maidman J, House R (2011). The bad faith of 'evidence-based practice': beyond counsels of despair. *Therapy Today 22*(6): 26–29.

Roth A, Hill A, Pilling S (2009). *The Competences Required to Deliver Effective Humanistic Psychological Therapies*. London: University College London.

Rupani P, Haughey N, Cooper M (2012). The impact of school-based counselling on young people's capacity to study and learn. *British Journal of Guidance & Counselling 40*(5): 499–514.

Rupani P, Cooper M, McArthur K, Pybis J, Cromarty K, Hill A, Levesley R, Murdoch J, Turner N (2014). The goals of young people in school-based counselling and their achievement of these goals. *Counselling and Psychotherapy Research 14*(4): 306–314. doi: 10.1080/14733145.2013.816758

Russell ST, Ryan C, Toomey RB, Diaz RM, Sanchez J (2011). Lesbian, gay, bisexual and transgender adolescent school victimization: implications for young adult health and adjustment. *Journal of School Health 81*(5): 223–230.

Sanders P (2006). *The Person-Centred Counselling Primer*. Ross-on-Wye: PCCS Books.

Smith B, Widdowson M (2003). Child-centred counselling. In: Lago C, Smith B (eds). *Anti-Discriminatory Practice in Counselling & Psychotherapy*. London: Sage.

Stalker K, McArthur K (2012). Child abuse, child protection and disabled children: a review of recent research. *Child Abuse Review 21*(1): 24–40.

Statistics for Wales (2016) *Counselling for Children and Young People 2014/15*. Experimental statistics. Cardiff: Statistics for Wales.

Suicide Prevention Resource Center (2008). *Suicide risk and prevention for lesbian, gay, bisexual, and transgender youth*. Newton, MA: Education Development Center Inc. www.sprc.org/library/SPRC_LGBT_Youth.pdf (accessed 20 February 2016).

Thompson CE, Jenal ST (1994). Interrracial and intraracial quasi-counseling interaction when counsellors avoid discussing race. *Journal of Counseling Psychology 41*: 484–491.

Tryon GS, Winograd G (2002). Goal consensus and collaboration. In: Norcross JC (ed). *Psychotherapy Relationships That Work*. New York: Oxford University Press (pp 109–125).

Twigg E, Cooper M, Evans C, Freire E, Mellor-Clark J, McInnes B, Barkham M (2015). Acceptability, reliability, referential distributions and sensitivity to change in the Young Person's Clinical Outcomes in Routine Evaluation (YP-CORE) outcome measure: replication and refinement. *Child and Adolescent Mental Health*. doi: 10.1111/camh.12128.

Wasserman D, Cheng Q, Jiang G (2005). Global suicide rates among young people aged 15–19. *World Psychiatry 4*(2): 114–120.

Watson V (2006). Key issues for black counselling practitioners in the UK, with particular reference to their experiences in professional training. In: Lago C (ed). *Race, Culture and Counselling: the ongoing challenge (2nd ed)*. Maidenhead: Open University Press (pp187–197).

Weissman M M, Wolk S, Goldstein RB, Moreau D, Adams P, Greenwald S, Klier CM, Ryan ND, Dahl RE, Wickramaratne P (1999). Depressed adolescents grown up. *Journal of the American Medical Association 281*: 1707–1713.

Weisz JR, Weiss B, Han SS, Granger D A, Morton T (1995). Effects of psychotherapy with children and adolescents revisited - a meta-analysis of treatment outcome studies. *Psychological Bulletin 117*(3): 450–468.

Wheeler S, Elliott R (2008). What do counsellors and psychotherapists need to know about research? *Counselling and Psychotherapy Research 8*(2): 133–135.

Wisdom J, Green C (2004). 'Being in a funk': teens' efforts to understand their depressive experiences. *Qualitative Health Research 14*(9): 1227–1238.

World Health Organization (2014). *Global Status Report on Noncommunicable Diseases*. Geneva: WHO. www.who.int/nmh/publications/ncd-status-report-2014/en/ (accessed 21 February 2016).

INDEX